NEW PENGUIN SHAKESPEARE

GENERAL EDITOR: T. J. B. SPENCER

ASSOCIATE EDITOR: STANLEY WELLS

WILLIAM SHAKESPEARE

✳

TITUS ANDRONICUS

INTRODUCTION AND COMMENTARY BY
JACQUES BERTHOUD

EDITED BY SONIA MASSAI

PENGUIN BOOKS

PENGUIN BOOKS

Published by the Penguin Group
Penguin Books Ltd, 80 Strand, London WC2R 0RL, England
Penguin Putnam Inc., 375 Hudson Street, New York, New York 10014, USA
Penguin Books Australia Ltd, 250 Camberwell Road, Camberwell, Victoria 3124, Australia
Penguin Books Canada Ltd, 10 Alcorn Avenue, Toronto, Ontario, Canada M4V 3B2
Penguin Books India (P) Ltd, 11 Community Centre, Panchsheel Park, New Delhi – 110 017, India
Penguin Books (NZ) Ltd, Cnr Rosedale and Airborne Roads, Albany, Auckland, New Zealand
Penguin Books (South Africa) (Pty) Ltd, 24 Sturdee Avenue, Rosebank 2196, South Africa

Penguin Books Ltd, Registered Offices: 80 Strand, London WC2R 0RL, England

www.penguin.com

This edition first published in Penguin Books 2001
5

Introduction and Commentary copyright © Jacques Berthoud, 2001
Further Reading and An Account of the Text copyright © Sonia Massai, 2001

Set in 10/11.75 pt PostScript Monotype Ehrhardt
Typeset by Rowland Phototypesetting Ltd, Bury St Edmunds, Suffolk
Printed in England by Clays Ltd, St Ives plc

CONTENTS

INTRODUCTION

I

It has taken nearly four hundred years for Shakespeare's first tragedy to recover its original credit. That it made an overwhelming impact when it appeared in the early 1590s is evident from the surviving record of performances both in the London theatres and in the household of Sir John Harington at Burley-on-the-Hill in Rutland on 1 January 1596. This popularity is also clear from the demand for 'the book of the play', which went into three quarto editions between 1594 and 1611 before its canonization in the definitive Folio of 1623; and also from miscellaneous printed evidence, such as a ballad, 'Titus Andronicus' Complaint', associated with the play's first success, and a passing reference by the 'bookkeeper' of Ben Jonson's *Bartholomew Fair*, produced in 1614, to an Andronicus fan club still alive and well 'some five and twenty, or thirty years' on. However, for a period of nearly three hundred years, stretching from the Restoration to the Second World War, *Titus Andronicus* was taken seriously only by a handful of textual and bibliographical scholars. Readers, when they could be found, mostly regarded it as a contemptible farrago of violence and bombast, while theatrical managers treated it either as a script in need of radical rewriting, or as a show-biz opportunity for a star actor, especially in the role of Aaron.

All this has changed. The reputation of *Titus Andronicus* – among directors, actors, critics, editors, academics, audiences and students – has never been higher since the play's heyday at the end of the sixteenth century. Theatrically, the turning point was Peter Brook's 1955 Stratford-upon-Avon production, with Laurence Olivier and Anthony Quayle beyond competition as Titus and Aaron, and a cut text projecting effects of barbaric violence and ritualized cruelty. This success prompted a sequence of independent productions by serious companies, which was brought to an unforgettable climax in Deborah Warner's uncut version – the first such since, presumably, the 1590s – at the Stratford Swan Theatre in 1987, which, without mitigating the play's ferocity, did full justice to its intellectual brilliance and social sophistication, but also to a richness of humanity that had still not yet been fully understood.

II

The first known performance of *Titus Andronicus* was given by Sussex's Men at the Rose Theatre on 24 January 1594. Performances were however soon suspended following a fresh outbreak of plague at the end of January. The play was entered in the Stationers' Register on 6 February 1594 and published shortly afterwards.

Both internal and external evidence suggests a slightly earlier date of composition. The title-page of the First Quarto, which appeared in 1594, carries the play's theatrical history thus: 'As it was Plaide by the Right Honourable the Earle of Darbie, Earle of Pembrooke, and the Earle of Sussex their Servants.' We have independent evidence that Pembroke's Men went bankrupt and ceased production in August 1593, and no sign of their existence predates 1592. We also know from strong circumstantial evidence that

Shakespeare had close associations with the company pro-
tected by the Earls of Derby. It is therefore reasonable to
assume that the title-page list is chronological, a fact that
gains yet further confirmation from the title-page of the
Second Quarto (1600), which, though repeating the list in
a slightly different order at a time when memories had
faded, brings the stage history up to date by printing last
the name of Shakespeare's current company, the famous
'Lorde Chamberlaine [his] Servants'; and by that of the
Third Quarto (1611) which now dispenses wholly with
ancient history in favour of the current holders of the play,
'the Kings Majesties Servants' – the name assumed by the
Lord Chamberlain's Men under James I.

An allusion to *Titus Andronicus* in a play called *A Knack
to Know a Knave* –

> *As welcome shall you be . . .*
> *As Titus was unto the Roman senators,*
> *When he had made a conquest on the Goths,*
> *That in requital of his service done,*
> *Did offer him the imperial diadem*

– also suggests a slightly earlier date of composition. This
memorially reconstructed text was first published in 1594,
but Philip Henslowe's Diary records seven performances
of *A Knack* by the Lord Strange's [or Admiral's] Men at
the Rose, between 9 and 12 June 1592 and 24 January
1593. I find unconvincing the claim that this near-exact
reference to the play could have been the result of a 1594
memorial confusion of the two texts; it is possible that
these lines could have been an insertion in *A Knack* to
advertise a new play by Shakespeare; but to me what they
seem to be doing is making opportunistic use for expressive
purposes of already well-known material; indeed they
assume the celebrity of a play which, as we have seen, was

still remembered by the audience of *Bartholomew Fair*. In this perspective, it would seem that *Titus Andronicus* must already have entered the repertoire of Derby's Men by the end of 1591 or the start of 1592 at the latest.

The plague continued to grip London for the whole of 1593, forcing the large urban companies to act before provincial audiences. Strange's Men had to appeal to the Privy Council for special treatment, and, as Henslowe reported to Alleyn in a letter of 23 September, Pembroke's Men collapsed altogether in mid-August, and were driven to pawn their costumes and sell their play-texts (including the titles mentioned above), in order to satisfy their creditors. This disastrous year also saw the twenty-nine-year-old Christopher Marlowe's violent death on 30 May, and Thomas Kyd's arrest and torture for alleged atheism, which precipitated his death fifteen months later at the age of thirty-six.

The third company to perform *Titus Andronicus*, Sussex's Men, had run uninterrupted under three earls from 1569. In the early nineties they had made one appearance at court, in 1591–2 when Strange's Men had shown their six plays. They seem to have survived 1593 better than most, for between 27 December of that year and 6 February of the next, they had a successful run at the Rose, with very profitable performances of *Titus Andronicus*, explicitly recorded by Henslowe as theirs, on 24 January, 28 January and 6 February – the very day on which the printer John Danter registered 'a booke intituled a Noble Roman Historye of Tytus Andronicus'. How did Sussex's Men gain the rights over the production of *Titus*? The most plausible story is that they picked up some actors and their plays from Pembroke's broken company. In any event, by the start of 1594 the whole system of play-production was coming apart. Sussex's patron, the 4th

Earl, had died just before the beginning of their run at the Rose, leaving their future uncertain. As for Derby's Men, they had been left destitute by the sudden death of their new patron, Lord Strange's son, Ferdinando Stanley, after only seven months. And to cap these disasters, on 6 February a further recrudescence of the plague once again closed the theatres.

When the epidemic finally lifted in April, the two theatre supremos, the Queen's Chamberlain Henry Carey Lord Hunsdon, who was responsible for ensuring court entertainment during the long Christmas season, and his son-in-law Charles Howard, himself a former Chamberlain and now Lord Admiral, decided to consolidate the best available dramatic talent into two strong companies. Hunsdon himself took charge of the first, which became known as The Chamberlain's Men. Made up of top actors from Strange's/Derby's Men and from Pembroke's Men, it was led by Richard Burbage, with William Shakespeare as resident playwright, and with 'The Theatre' – soon to be rebuilt as 'The Globe' – as its playhouse. Hence Shakespeare's entire corpus, *Titus Andronicus* included, passed into the new company's control. The second company, under Howard, became the new Admiral's Men, with Edward Alleyn as their star actor, Marlowe's plays as their prestige repertoire and Henslow's 'Rose' as their base.

Thus ended what could be called the heroic phase of Elizabethan drama, in which *Titus Andronicus* occupied a central place. The appearance of Marlowe's two *Tamburlaine* plays and Thomas Kyd's *Spanish Tragedie* in *c.* 1587–8 unlocked the theatrical energies that had been intermittently building up since Thomas More's play-writing circle under Henry VIII. As Marlowe's *Dr Faustus* and *The Jew of Malta* (*c.* 1589–91) show, traditional genres were stunningly revitalized or transformed. But what dominated this seven-year phase was a succession of increasingly powerful and ambitious historico-tragic dramas, with escalating casts and a growing ability to represent collective life on stage. These plays, which all have demonstrable connections with *Titus Andronicus*, included: Thomas Lodge's *The Wounds of Civil War* (*c.* 1589) staging the conflict between Marius and Sulla (the first surviving theatrical depiction of Roman history); George Peele's *The Battle of Alcazar* (*c.* 1589) and Marlowe's *Massacre at Paris* (*c.* 1592), the first dramatizations of near-contemporary real-life events (respectively the catastrophic destruction of the Portuguese by the Moroccan Moors in 1578, and the St Bartholomew's Eve massacre of French Huguenots in 1572); Robert Greene's *Selimus* (*c.* 1591) evoking the murderous dynastic rivalries of the Ottoman sultinate in the Turkey of 1512; and most of all the English history plays: Shakespeare's *Henry VI* trilogy (1591–2) and Marlowe's *Edward II* (*c.* 1591–2). These wonderfully productive six or seven years found perhaps their most characteristic expression in a dramatic form that could be called tragical history, and of which Shakespeare's *Titus Andronicus* (1591) and *Richard III* (1592–3) are the supreme instances.

III

In 1589 a twenty-year-old Thomas Nashe launched an attack on playwrights who 'could scarcely Latinise their neck verse if they should have need' – that is to say, who were barely able to convert into Latin the biblical verse proving they could claim 'benefit of clergy' and so escape the gallows; or who ransacked 'English Seneca . . . by candlelight' for 'many good sentences' (quotations); or who at a moment's notice would supply 'handfuls of tragical speeches' ('To the Gentlemen Students of Both Universities', *Works*, ed. R. B. McKerrow and F. P. Wilson, Oxford University Press, 1958, vol. 3, pp. 315–16). Various puns and allusions make it clear that Nashe's particular target was Thomas Kyd, who, like Shakespeare, presumed to write plays without the advantage of a university degree, and who, incapable of distinguishing Rome from England or evil from good, 'thrust Elysium into hell' – a phrase maliciously culled from *The Spanish Tragedie*.

In such a context there can be little doubt that despite his phenomenal early success Shakespeare had something to prove. *Titus Andronicus* was the first of a group of Rome-inspired texts, which included *Venus and Adonis* (1592–3), *The Rape of Lucrece* (1593–4) and *The Comedy of Errors* (1594). These works, however, represent a challenge less to Shakespeare's contemporaries (the so-called 'university wits' championed by the precocious Nashe) than to antiquity itself. The two narrative poems comprehensively outdo their Latin sources, Ovid's *Metamorphoses* X and his *Fasti* II, in their elaboration of emotional conflict. *The Comedy of Errors* adds a second pair of identical twins to Plautus's *Menachmi* to complicate the source plot by a factor of four. *Titus Andronicus* not only introduces one of its main 'sources', the Philomela episode of *Metamorphoses* VI into the narrative – to the point of bringing Ovid's very book on stage – but, as we shall see, explicitly improves on it. In Ovid, Pandion, King of Athens, gives his daughter Procne to Tereus, King of Thrace, for saving Athens; Tereus takes her back to his country, and a son, Itys, is born of the marriage. After five years, Procne persuades Tereus to fetch her sister Philomela from Athens for a visit. Tereus falls insanely but secretly in love with her. Pandion entrusts his second daughter to him; but when they reach Thrace, Tereus takes her to a 'hut deep hidden in the ancient woods'. She pleads for mercy, then for death. Incensed, he rapes her repeatedly and cuts out her tongue. He then leaves her under guard, returns to Procne and pretends that Philomela is dead. In the ensuing year, Philomela stitches the story of her wrongs in a tapestry and sends it to Procne. Under cover of the wild festival of Bacchus celebrated by the uninhibited Thracian women, Procne finds Philomela in the woods and brings her back home disguised as a bacchante. Uncovering the 'shame-blanched face' of her sister, she becomes deranged with hate for Tereus. She notices that her small son Itys looks like his father, represses her maternal love, cuts his throat like 'a tigress', and cooks him, offering him to Tereus as part of a sacred feast. Having 'gorged himself with the flesh of his own flesh', he calls for Itys, only to receive the reply 'You have, within, him whom you want', while Philomela thrusts the boy's head into his face. Beside himself with rage and grief, Tereus pursues Pandion's daughters with drawn sword. As they flee, Philomela turns into a nightingale, Procne into a swallow and Tereus into a hoopoe. In *Titus Andronicus*, it is the self-conscious Aaron who proposes to out-do Ovid, both in ingenuity (doubling the mutilations) and in rhetoric (by turning art into life); but it is Titus who in his turn will eventually overtake him in both departments.

Shakespeare was, as it were, competing with Rome, not with Nashe, or Greene – who, three years after Nashe, was himself to attack Shakespeare as 'the only Shake-scene in the country' in his *Greene's Groat's-Worth of Witte 1592* (literally reprinted by G. B. Harrison in *Elizabethan and Jacobean Quartos*, Edinburgh University Press, 1967, pp. 45–6). It almost seems as if Shakespeare's response to humanist snobbery was to set up a premature quarrel of the ancients and the moderns, in order to demonstrate the superiority of the latter. If the depth and intensity of Shakespeare's interest in Rome as such is still under question after this first classical phase, it is put beyond doubt by his second, when his encounter with Plutarch produced three masterpieces, *Julius Caesar* (1599), *Antony and Cleopatra* (1606) and *Coriolanus* (1608), which have never been equalled in their capacity to resurrect, without the faintest taint of antiquarianism or pedantry, Rome and its Romans on the modern stage.

Titus Andronicus is not, of course, in any sense a Plutarchian play. Its principal model is probably a pseudo-historical prose narrative which resurfaced between 1736 and 1764 under the title 'The History of Titus Andronicus ... Newly Translated from the Italian Copy printed at Rome'. The nineteenth-century Shakespearean scholar J. O. Halliwell-Phillips reported that he owned a version of this history. The only surviving copy is now in the Folger Library, Washington. There is no compelling reason for ruling out the existence of an Italian source. Renaissance Italy was very interested in the history of the later Roman empire, and Italian translations of virtually all the major Greek sources were available. Nor is there any special reason to question the claim of the eighteenth-century pamphlet's publisher that it represented a new, or at least revised, translation. Of course, the existence of such a source in Elizabethan translation would not bring greater discredit to *Titus* than Arthur Brooke's 'Tragicall Historye of Romeus and Juliet', ultimately derived from the Italian, brought to Shakespeare's next tragedy, *Romeo and Juliet*. Moreover, the existence of such a source would in no way diminish our perception of Shakespeare's creative engagement with his predecessors, though it would not lend support to the magpie version of that engagement, which represents the playwright as collecting bits and pieces of narrative material from a whole variety of sources until they spontaneously cohered to form a new narrative. What it would do, however, is to explain why, unlike Lodge's *Wounds of Civil War* or Shakespeare's own later Roman plays, *Titus Andronicus* fails to recreate a specific period of Roman history – or rather why it creates an historical hybrid, combining the stern republican Rome of Cato the Elder with the third-century imperial Rome of, say, the emperors Decius and Severus, with its internal persecutions and its frontiers permeable to Gothic invaders who, even then, were starting to assimilate the civilization of their victims. Yet for all its apparent chronological irresponsibility, *Titus* provides astonishing evidence of the depth of Shakespeare's imaginative assimilation of Rome and its culture.

Explanations of Shakespeare's powers of assimilation must start with the recognition that his historical drama is much more 'sociological' or 'anthropological' than moral or political. Of course Shakespeare is not lacking in political or moral concepts; but if plays like *Titus Andronicus* or the stupendous *Coriolanus* are political, they are so more by virtue of their awareness of how political projects are formed and conducted than for their endorsement of this or that political programme. The evolution of the historical play over the seven years that followed the appearance of *Tamburlaine I* (1587) was essentially a movement from a conception of society as docile before individual will to one of society as resistant to it.

The simultaneous movement of late Elizabethan drama towards such a relativized conception of character is owed as much to dramaturgical developments as to new conceptions of the relationship of the self to the social. Much the most important of the former is the emergence of interactive dialogue as a theatrical norm. In a play like *Gorboduc* (1561), by no means a contemptible text, the dialogue for the most part takes the form of speeches describing off-stage events which could be addressed equally to other actors or the audience, in order to enforce a lesson: that unless the Queen begets an heir or appoints a successor, the realm of England will disintegrate. With the appearance of *Tamburlaine*, speeches given and received become expressions of a mighty personality whose existence evolves in its relation to the other members of the cast, but only in order to dominate them by seduction or authority or terror. With *Titus Andronicus* (*c.*1591–2), however, the entire dramatic script, soliloquies included, functions as a network of responses and reactions. Although the language of the play of course exhibits more formal registers – symbolic, ritualistic, intertextual – its primary and consistent function is interlocutory.

How far and deep this goes can be demonstrated from its most stylized scene, Act 2, scene 4, in which Titus's brother, Marcus, finds his niece Lavinia wandering in the forest chase outside Rome, having been raped and mutilated by the sons of the Gothic queen, Tamora. Confronted by the appalling spectacle, Marcus notoriously launches into a 47–line allegedly Ovidian speech which seems to defy every convention of interactive realism. What accord can there be between Lavinia's monstrous disfigurement and Marcus's display of verbal luxuriance? Each, it appears, makes the other unacceptable: her pain turns his fluency into an affront; his verbiage demeans her suffering; and the scene between them becomes humanly trivial and theatrically chilled. For many, as for Peter Brook who simply omitted Marcus's speech from his historic 1955 production, it is unrescuable. For others, salvaging it can only be accomplished indirectly. Here, the standard line of defence has been that the speech is not a dramatic failure because it was never designed to be a dramatic success. Thus, in *Shakespeare's Early Tragedies* (1968), Nicholas Brooke wrote: 'Lavinia is turned into a stone in the formalized language of the poetry . . . [She] is dumb and unmoving like the woodcuts in an emblem book, while Marcus provides the interpretative verses that were usually printed beneath.' Stage animation is petrified into a tableau, and the momentum of dialogue suspended into a commentary. Still more ingeniously, the play's distinguished (1984) Oxford editor, Eugene Waith, claimed that what Marcus is trying to bring about, through sheer force of incantation, is an Ovidian metamorphosis, transforming a brutalized scenario into a pastoral idyll, but that he is checked by the reality of the woman before him – the literal refusing conversion into the metaphorical. Finally, and most recently, in an ambitious book entitled *Shakespeare's Troy* (1997), Heather James reads the play as an Ovidian 'deformation' of conservative Virgilian eloquence, arguing that Shakespeare 'transforms Lavinia's body into a site for a skeptical analysis of metaphor'. In the *Aeneid*, Virgil's Dido, sexual victim of the imperializing Aeneas, is absorbed into the imperialist project by virtue of a noble style that refuses to call a seduction a seduction. In the *Metamorphoses*, Ovid applies the epic simile to Philomela's rape, but only to show up its inability to ennoble Tereus's contemptible act. In *Titus Andronicus*, Shakespeare associates Lavinia's and thus Philomela's rape with Dido's seduction, thereby showing up the latter as 'a scene of violation [sic] in which responsibility cannot be obscured' (p. 63). The moral responsibility in question is Aeneas's, for in *this* reading of Virgil, it is only Dido who has been seduced. The general argument is as such intelligible: the imperial idea travels west, from Troy to Rome and from

Rome to Britain. Shakespeare is an anti-imperialist, so he writes a play proving that Aeneas was no better than a rapist, and that the Elizabethan establishment is immoral. The question is, however, one of plausibility.

What these readings, culled from three decades of commentary, overlook is the fact that a play is primarily dialogic – for example, that Marcus is first and foremost addressing his niece. What Marcus's speech offers is in fact a highly original form of interactive dialogue in which one party cannot speak and the other, perforce, cannot hear. This means that the sub-text – the stage direction implied in the spoken text – becomes hyperactive. Marcus enters 'from hunting'. His first line (11) shows that Lavinia is trying to avoid being seen. His next line (12) tells us not only that she stops and turns, but why she does so: Marcus's enquiry as to the whereabouts of Bassianus touches a reflex need to report his murder. But in turning she has revealed her visible mutilations. Marcus's change of tone (from 12 to 13) shows that he has fully registered the shock of her condition. Appalled at the discovery that she is without hands (13–15), he asks her to reveal the name of the perpetrator (16–21). Her silence prompts him to ask again (21). Her effort to reply causes a fresh haemorrhage, which shows him the extent of her physical mutilation (22–5) and provokes him to guess the reason for it (26–7). She turns away in shame, which confirms his insight (28–32); so she allows him to come closer to her (33–7) and, as Donald Sumpter did in Deborah Warner's revelatory production, to hold her (38–43), and even cradle her in his arms (44–51). He ends by raising her to lead her to her father (52–5); she shrinks back at the prospect (56), but finally yields to his persuasion (57). That this is a scene consisting of two characters reacting and responding to each other must surely put pay to claims that Lavinia is turned into an emblem and her sufferings into a ritual.

If Lavinia, at least in the theatre, is neither a motionless image in need of commentary (Brooke), nor a broken body provoking a vain lyricism of healing (Waith), nor even an emblem of the true meaning of the poetic blazon (James), we are still left with Marcus's expressive volubility. That, dramatically speaking, it is seen to be as problematic as Lavinia's silence can be detected in the fear of commentators that any attempt to 'humanize' Marcus will reveal him to be little better than a talking machine, or an unperceiving sentimentalist, or an unfeeling Ovidian lyricist. But even a simple review of his speech in the context of an interactive relationship will, I think, show these anxieties to be misplaced. His first two lines (11–12) are cast in the language of normal life which takes for granted ordinary familial relations ('niece', 'cousin', 'husband'). This tone is required for the concussive change of register of the next three lines (13–15), which express his sense of cosmic dislocation ('dream', 'wake', 'planet'). In his next six lines (16–21), he asks for the identity of her assailant; but he does so with an overpowering sense of the irreparability and the incomprehensibility of what that assailant has done. This is effected through the conceit of disbranching, which conveys not only the brutality ('lopped', 'hewed') but the perversion of the deed: some 'stern ungentle hands' cutting off gentle, sensitive hands, and thus extinguishing the 'beauty' and 'happiness' of a life-restoring embrace ('circling shadows'). The following six lines (22–27), which enact the discovery of her further mutilation and rape begin by horribly heightening the sense of a perverted nature (a wind-stirred water-spring as a bubbling 'river of warm blood'), prompting him to summon the figure of Tereus, here less a 'literary allusion' to Ovid than an inspired guess which Marcus communicates to her in the literal plainness of

> But sure some Tereus has deflowered thee,
> And, lest thou shouldst detect him, cut thy tongue.

The next five lines (28–32) evoking Lavinia's gestures of shame, release in their sudden baroque extravagance (blood pouring out of the open taps of her wounds, her face suffused with redness like a sky) a recognition of the enormity of what has happened to her, and by implication to him.

Marcus's response to Lavinia's state exhibits two qualities seldom found together: an unevasive emotional recognition of the horror of her injuries, and the knowledge that, despite her transformation into a living grave of herself, she remains the person he knows and loves. He may not possess her story ('O that I knew thy heart', 34), but his protective identification with her, which the rest of his speech dramatizes, never wavers. In the five lines (33–7) that express the pain of blocked grief, the distinctions between his heart-burning (37) and hers, and between speaking on his own and on her behalf (33) become blurred. This sets the course for the rest of his speech, in which he offers her the consolation of a full knowledge of what she has lost, and thereby of her continuing worth. In his next six lines (38–43), he not only recognizes that her suffering is worse than 'fair' Philomela's, but also that her beauty ('lovely niece') and accomplishments outstripped her Ovidian predecessor's. Because Marcus does not minimize the significance of what has happened to her, he enables her to re-approach the familial household of which she feels herself to have become unworthy. Hence his next eight lines (44–51) are able to bring this process of reclamation to some sort of conclusion. The 'beast' (34) who cut off the 'pretty fingers' (42) of the embroiderer becomes the 'monster' (44) who tears off the hands and tongue of the singer-lutenist. In such a context, the comparison of Lavinia and her ravisher to Orpheus and Cerberus must and does remain a conceit. She is indeed a wondrous musician both literally (45) and symbolically (48); but in the world of this play, where there is no second chance, the 'silken strings' can offer no resistance to the chopper. With the six-line coda (52–7) of, as it were, Marcus's monologue of two – in this reading one of the memorable expressions of protective love in Shakespeare – he achieves the only victory available to him: coaxing his niece, despite her last recoil, to accept the community of woe (see III.1.148) that their family is becoming: 'Do not draw back, for we will mourn for thee' – even as he knows that such a comfort cannot repair the irreparable: 'O, could our mourning ease thy misery.'

IV

Interactive dialogue enacts one of the ways in which individuals can be imagined to exist in society. In so far as they are the centre of their own lives, individuals belong to themselves; but in so far as they are members of a community, with its history, its institutions and its social and cultural divisions, they belong to others. The kind of dramatic dialogue we have been examining expresses such a community, not discursively or analytically, but at the moment of its operation. It is therefore the least abstract representation of social life we possess. No play deserves the name that does not in some measure display this property. Ritualistic or religious drama tends to blend conflicting points of view into a single vision; naturalistic drama, on the other hand, tends to treat such differences deterministically, as the products of society, and history; yet both depend on actors capable of reacting to one another. Such homogenizing tendencies, however, are absent from the finest plays of the London stage of the early 1590s. They distinguish between the individual and the social, of course, but that distinction is perspectival: that is to say, it permits two equally valid descriptions of the same piece of dialogue – as the expression of individual agency, and as the reflection of social process. On *that* stage, every utterance is simultaneously a message and a symptom.

Even in the scene between Marcus and Lavinia, in which one party is mute, and during which both are drawn together into the solidarity of grief, we remain aware of discrepant consciousnesses. Just as our perception of Lavinia's state is variously intensified by Marcus's responses to her, as his predicament is by her reactions, so we cannot but become aware that together they reveal the marks of a recognizable social group. For example, whether we are conscious of it or not, we very early register the fact that they are patricians. The traumatized Lavinia is introduced into the play, as 'Rome's rich ornament' (Bassianus, I.1.55), and her subsequent conduct shows her as being confident and at ease in that role. It is in part because of this loss of status that initially she shrinks from her uncle. Marcus, civilized, self-possessed, sympathetic and rational, is appalled by the surgery that has been practised on her body. His instinct is to draw her into the protective resources of the Roman family; but even so, his consciousness of defeat is palpable, particularly as one begins to be aware that he laments the destruction of talent and beauty not only for her sake, but also for his own as an Andronicus and a Roman.

That the effects of interactive dialogue extend beyond the personal to the social becomes overwhelmingly apparent as soon as we locate Lavinia and Marcus's encounter within the whole of the scene. Marcus's speech is prefaced by an infernal duet between Demetrius and Chiron, the perpetrators of the outrage, who have been egged on by Aaron and Tamora to rape and maim the young woman Tamora has called 'this trull' (II.3.191). Having made Lavinia safe, the brothers can now gloat over their handiwork. They are provoked into crass inventiveness by their discovery that her mutilations have turned normal language into nonsense. For example, Chiron's 'Go home, call for sweet water, wash thy hands', prompts Demetrius's

> *She hath no tongue to call, nor hands to wash,*
> *And so let's leave her to her silent walks.*   (II.4.6–8)

These loutish exchanges are obviously venomous with misogyny. What is less obvious, but quite as brutal, is their class hatred: 'Sweet water' is perfumed water, 'silent walks' are solitary walks, in the quiet part of a garden, for the purposes of meditation. These are plainly aristocratic practices, and they drive these Goths, at once spoilt and half-educated, into a frenzy of aggression. It seems scarcely extravagant to suggest that the author of this play may at such moments have remembered the sack of Rome, either of AD 410 (by the Visigoths) or of 1527 (by the Germans). Be that as it may, my point is that his capacity to see through the eyes of a particular character gives him, by virtue of the fact that there is always more than one character, his point of entry into the forms of life that this individual perspective implies. One of the effects of the opening ten lines on the rest of the scene is to establish a relativity of perspectives that allows the playwright to make the barbarian status of these 'Goths' as perceptible as the patrician status of those 'Romans'.

The notoriety of *Titus Andronicus* as the most violent of all Elizabethan plays has (if my dating is right) concealed its importance as the first sustained attempt to put a consistent foreign world on the stage. Despite occasional anachronisms mostly Christian, and almost entirely associated with Aaron, who attracts them because he raises the problem of 'irreligiousness', or what we would now call atheism – problems which cannot readily be dramatized, or even imagined, in relation to Jupiter or Diana – Shakespeare's re-creation of pagan antiquity takes dramatic art on to a new level of mimetic sophistication. In this respect it far outstrips Lodge's *Wounds of Civil War*, which competently translates Appian's *Civil Wars* into the staged rivalries of Marius and Sulla, or Greene's *Selimus*, which portrays Islamic Turkey as some sort of hell of competing dynastic ambitions within a geography of resonant place-names. The crucial point of difference is not how well Shakespeare's knowledge of Roman life compares with our own stock of accumulated hindsight, but the degree to which he has been able to imagine a different form of life *from the inside*.

What this achievement entails can be illustrated from his use of so-called classical allusions which he deploys more liberally in *Titus* than in any other of his plays. A comparison with Marlowe's use of such allusions is instructive. Try to strike me, Tamburlaine tells Theridamas, who has been charged by the King of Persia to put an end to the banditry of the Scythian shepherd, 'And Jove himself will stretch his hand from heaven | To ward the blow'. This is the brilliant new language of hyperbolic glamour. It does not disclose Tamburlaine's religious allegiances, but merely embodies his sense, and ours, of

his effortless power. Shakespeare's Titus, who does not
keep his victories for himself but brings them back to
Rome, also invokes Jove:

> *Thou great defender of this Capitol,*
> *Stand gracious to the rites that we intend.*

(I.1.80–81)

Titus's Jove is Jupiter Capitolinus – not a verbal gesture,
or even a symbol, but a god, the object of specific 'rites' of
worship, the recipient of prayers of intercession, the owner
of a great temple which is the historical and religious centre
of the city, and which Titus sees before him as he speaks
('*this* Capitol'). The difference between the two playwrights is not, of course, that Shakespeare is a better
Roman historian than Marlowe, the translator of Lucan's
Pharsalia and Ovid's *Amores*; it is that Rome is inside
Shakespeare's Titus as well as outside of him, or more
explicitly, that Titus contains much more of his environment than Marlowe's Tamburlaine does of his. The fact
not merely of an interdependence, but of an interaction,
between the individual and the social – the fact that the
individual lives in society to the extent to which society
lives in him – distinguishes of course human from natural
communities such as the bee-swarm or the sardine-school,
where the life of the collectivity is identical to that of the
collected.

The way in which the characters of *Titus Andronicus*
invoke their classical and Roman past shows that they are
its product. That past is astonishingly comprehensive,
descending, as it does, from the pre-Olympian and
Olympian gods (Ovid), to the Trojan founders of Rome
(Virgil), to the creators of the Republic (Livy) and the
degenerates of Empire (Suetonius). We can only glance at
a couple of examples. As early as line 23 of the play,

the incorruptibly humane tribune, Marcus, introduces his brother, the incorruptibly valorous general Titus, as 'Andronicus, surnamed Pius' – the honorary epithet bestowed by Virgil on Aeneas, and by Aeneas on his deserving successors. Titus himself, by virtue of his ten-year defence of Rome against the Goths, which has cost him the lives of twenty-one out of his twenty-five sons – 'Half of the number that King Priam had' (I.1.83) – proclaims his descent from that heroic ancestry. By the middle of the play, three more of Titus's sons having met summary executions (two by edict of the Senate, one at his own hand), his sole surviving son Lucius, having been unjustly banished, raises an army of disaffected Goths in the name of ancient virtue, and takes over Rome. At the end of the play, the continuity affirmed at its start is re-established. Marcus, once again, enrolls him in the same succession as his father, as 'the Roman Hector' (IV.1.87) and 'our ancestor [Aeneas]' (V.3.79). In general, Roman *integritas* is achieved by keeping alive the past in the present.

It cannot be an accident, therefore, that at the very climax of the play's denouement, Titus chooses to give the decadent Saturninus a lesson in the meaning of Roman history. Having, with the veiled Lavinia's help, served his guests, Titus turns to the head of state:

> *My lord the Emperor, resolve me this:*
> *Was it well done of rash Virginius*
> *To slay his daughter with his own right hand*
> *Because she was enforced, stained, and deflowered?*

SATURNINUS

> *It was, Andronicus.*

TITUS

> *Your reason, mighty lord?*

27

SATURNINUS

> *Because the girl should not survive her shame,*
> *And by her presence still renew his sorrows.*

TITUS

> *A reason mighty, strong, and effectual;*
> *A pattern, precedent, and lively warrant*
> *For me, most wretched, to perform the like.*

And he does. The parallel is not perfect. In Livy the centurion Virginius kills his daughter before, and not after the rape threatened by the ruthless *decemvir* Appius Claudius. (But see the explanatory note to V.3.36, and note.) However, as Livy himself observes, Virginia's killing became as exemplary as Lucrece's suicide, both events testifying to the austere virtue on which Rome's greatness was thought to rest. Titus, as embodiment of this virtue, kills not one but two of his children: Mutius, in the name of absolute paternal authority (but also in unconscious terror that his elevation of Saturninus to the purple is undoing Rome) at the beginning of the play, and Lavinia, in the name of female chastity, at the end. Saturninus as a Roman knows the story of Virginia, but a story is all it is to him. A free-thinking epicure and sensualist in a position that enables him to satisfy his every impulse, he cannot take seriously a fable that would cast him in the role of a Tarquin or an Appius Claudius. Thus, at the play's defining moment, Titus confronts Saturninus as Rome confronting Rome; and just as the deaths of Lucrece and Virginia once led to the banishment of kings and executive magistrates, so the killing of Lavinia sets off a cascade of executions that sweeps the Gothicized court out of Italy.

This triumph of ancestral Roman virtue does not mean, however, that Shakespeare has given up the irony inherent in his dramaturgy. The presence of a division within Rome between two sorts of Roman, the traditional and the modern, already signals that *Titus* as a text will not easily be hospitable to simple affirmations. This is reinforced by the fact that the restoration of Roman virtue requires the assistance of a Gothic army, which in turn suggests that the idea of the 'Gothic' is not a unitary one either. *Romanitas* itself, however, is more subtly destabilized by the way in which foreigners like the Gothic queen Tamora and her Moorish agent-lover Aaron, both of whom have acquired a veneer of Latin culture, invoke Roman history. Aeneas may be the founding father of Rome, but he has attributes other than piety – sexual passion, for example. This is noticed by the enamoured Tamora, now Roman empress, who invites her lover Aaron to an erotic 'conflict' – her word – 'such as was supposed | The wand'ring prince [Aeneas] and Dido once enjoyed' (II.3.21–2). The sceptical precision of that 'was supposed' should not be overlooked: Tamora may be a naturalized Roman, but her Gothic roots are alive and well. Not only is she drawn to the transgressive aspects of Virgil's great epic, but she maintains an emotional distance from its imperial claims. She displays a similar scepticism towards classical myth. When, for instance, she threatens the doomed Bassianus with 'Had I the power that *some say* Dian had' (II.3.61), it is Diana's divinity as well as her chastity that she despises.

Aaron's use of classical names is different again. Plays set in Islamic locations, such as *Selimus* or *The Battle of Alcazar*, use classical allusions in a routine way, generally to give an overall and undiscriminating colouring of non-Christianity – for instance, 'Latona's son' (73) and 'Bellona' (729) for 'the sun' or 'war' in *Selimus*, or 'Phlege-ton' (177) and 'Erebus' (1136) for 'hell' in *Alcazar*. Shakespeare eschews such one-dimensional usages in the speech he gives his Aaron. Aaron's classical deities, which he calls

29

on at moments of aggressive self-definition, are primitive, violent and obscure: Tamora is sexually bound to him like the tortured 'Prometheus tied to Caucasus' (II.1.17); his 'desires' are dominated by the grisly Saturn (II.3.31); he swears to keep his black child against the assaults of Enceladus (IV.2.92), the largest of the giants, whose breath fired Etna. Like his self-image (the black panther), his pantheon antedates human society, reaching back to an era of 'big-boned men framed of the Cyclops' size' – to cite Titus's granite-like phrase (IV.3.47). In this play, even the language of the classical past, which had long been the mythological lingua franca of Europe, becomes incorrigibly perspectival.

V

Shakespeare's attempt to imagine Roman culture from the inside is of course that of a man whose orientation is Tudor–Christian. In culturally naïve writers, who take their own environment as the norm of reality, the imagining of another world retains no essential distinguishing marks, and achieves no genuine otherness. Such writers cannot solve the problem by seeking to become culturally neutral. On the contrary, it is precisely because of his grip on his own social perspective that Shakespeare is able to perceive Rome as something other. Shakespeare's England is part of the differential equation. But his Rome is also distinguished internally in various ways, notably by means of the inclusion of an alien presence – though scarcely a culture in its own right – in the form of the Gothic captives.

Nothing testifies more subtly to Shakespeare's instinctive grasp of the essentials of *romanitas* than his placement of the Andronici's mortuary monument within the entrance to his play. No victorious return to Rome is less triumphalist than Titus's. Following the coffins of his dead sons, he greets Rome as if his bereavement were inseparable from hers; he calls on the graciousness of Jupiter; he opens the tomb that contains his earliest ancestors and their descendants, including his score of sons killed in previous campaigns; he ritually sacrifices a prisoner; and he completes the ceremony with a petitionary prayer echoed by his daughter (I.1.73–171).

In just under a hundred powerful lines, Shakespeare has established ancestor worship as the defining principle of the patrilineal Roman family. The tomb of the Andronici unites the living and the dead in a single community. Both rely on each other for pacification and fulfilment: without the performance of prescribed rites (which, according to Fustel de Coulanges's classic study, *La Cité Antique*, first published in 1864, included in primitive times the slaughter of horses and slaves to serve the dead) the dead would continue to 'hover on the dreadful shore of Styx' (91) while the living would be 'disturbed with prodigies on earth' (104). The continuity of their history would be broken. Titus receives his authority as priest and father from this monument, which he tends as a sacred duty that he calls a 'cell of virtue and nobility' (96; where 'cell' evokes the Roman 'cella', the body of the temple as opposed to its portico), and which had stood for five hundred years before he 're-edified' it (353–4). It is by virtue of this office that he embodies the family honour and upholds the family name, that he serves Rome and the gods with unswerving fidelity, and that he retains the power of life and death over his dependants. Later in the scene his consent is required before even Mutius, the son who resisted him and paid the penalty, is allowed to enter into the immortality of the monument. The traditional Roman was bound by a sacred tie to his 'house' and its 'sacred receptacle' (95), as to his City and its Capitol (80), both of which are addressed by name in Titus's salutation speech. This meant that sacredness was linked to a specific spot on the face of the earth. Thus to die in defence of one's 'altars and fires' (*pro aris et focis*) was the supreme mark of piety. In such a context, exile became the cruellest chastisement, for to be banished from 'home' was to be excluded from community not only in life but for ever. More than a trace of this can be found in Lucius's exile, to which he is sentenced in part fulfilment of the Tamora–Saturninus plot to 'raze' the Andronicus 'faction and . . . family' out of Rome (454). In their vindication speeches to the Roman people after the *coup d'état*, Marcus and Lucius allude to exile as the worst of fates, the one evoking 'a forlorn and desperate castaway' driven to doing 'shameless execution on himself' (V.3.74–5), the other describing himself as 'unkindly [unnaturally] banishèd, | The gates shut on me and turned weeping out' (V.3.103–4).

The Andronici in general, and Titus in particular, represent the persistence, within decadent imperial Rome, of traditions of ancient virtue receding into the penumbra of prehistory. But the play's mighty opening scene no sooner presents these traditions than it drives them to their limits by making the funeral rites which Titus performs include human sacrifice. As we have just seen, in ancestor worship the dead retain a form of existence responsive to the ministrations of the living. As his dead brothers are about to be consigned to the family sepulchre, Titus's eldest son, Lucius, demands the life of 'the proudest prisoner of the Goths' (I.1.99) as a sacrifice *ad manes fratrum* ('to the sacred shades of our brothers'). Overriding the pleas of the Gothic queen, Titus grants the brothers Tamora's eldest son Alarbus, who is summarily killed, cut into parts and burnt.

It has been argued that Shakespeare could not have written this scene (but Peele, we are told, could), or that he invented an anthropology that had no precedent in Rome. Both claims are surely mistaken. Shakespeare took this barbaric rite seriously enough to treat it as normal Roman, and even more normal British, practice at the end of one of his last plays, *Cymbeline* (V.5.70–80). Moreover, the literature of antiquity offered several cases, notably in the *Iliad* (the funeral of Patroclus, XXIII.158–60) and in the *Aeneid* (the funeral of Pallas, XI.81). Tamora's passionate maternal pleas, inviting the patristic Titus to share her perception of her child's fate, and concluding with the very argument which Portia would use to launch her appeal to Shylock's mercy (*The Merchant of Venice*, IV.1.184–97), makes any identification of Titus's perspective with Shakespeare's impossible to sustain. The sacrifice of Alarbus marks the limiting point of the lineage-family because to that family it is the fulfilment of its identity (the link between the dead and the living is preserved) while representing its contradiction (one family's piety is another's atrocity). Once again, the audience is placed simultaneously inside and outside a given perspective, the only difference being that now it is the perspective of a clan rather than of an individual. In Shakespeare's dramaturgy, all points of view, whether individual or collective, carry their cultural horizons with them.

Traditional Rome is in deep trouble in this play. Internally, it appears to be falling apart. There are three candidates for the 'diadem' (Saturninus, Bassianus and Titus) and three methods of choice (primogeniture, electoral college, plebiscite). The method favoured by traditionalists – primogeniture – produces Saturninus, an unstable hysteric. On the Roman frontier, despite Titus's repeated victories, the human cost of defence has become intolerable. Titus's grand entry (in Olivier's rendering of it) brings into view a 'battered veteran', whose every word seems to be 'dredged up from an ocean-bed of fatigue' (Kenneth Tynan, *Curtains*, 1961, pp. 103–5), and whose subsequent decisions in Act I, scene 1 – the summary rejection of Tamora's pleas (124–32), the wilful appointment of Saturninus to the purple (206–36), the reckless promise of Lavinia to him (237–60), the savage slaying of Mutius (280–95) – all reinforce the impression of disintegrating control. What are the reasons for this breakdown? Is it that traditional Rome has failed to respond to the pluralism of Empire? That it has clung too long to its absolute sense of identity, refusing to accept its place on the expanding map of the world it has created?

This extra-Roman world is represented in the play by the Goths, who appear in two guises. The Gothic army which the exiled Lucius joins, and which restores the Andronici to power in Rome is 'warlike' (II.1.61, IV.4.110, V.2.113, V.3.27) – an epithet which Lucius himself receives (IV.4.69). What we see of them shows that they are respectful of military prowess (V.1.9–11, 20), secure in the simple integrity and vigour of their northern fields and forests (V.1.14–15, 19, 20–21), and sturdily contemptuous of tyrants. (V.1.12, 16). These Goths are Germans, descendants of those tribes depicted by Tacitus in his *Germania*; and in supporting the Andronici's political cause, they share the values of the common Romans, who, like the compassionate Messenger who returns Titus's severed hand to him, along with the heads of his two sons, grow increasingly restive under Saturninus's incompetent tyrannical rule (IV.4.73–80).

But there is, of course, another group of Goths – as different from the soldier Goths as Saturninus is from Titus – which is given a much higher profile in the play.

The defining adjective for them is provided, appropriately enough, by Marcus who, with his equally rational but tougher nephew, Lucius, will help keep the play from spilling into a carnival of butchery. Pleading for the burial of Mutius, he reminds Titus: 'Thou art a Roman; be not barbarous' (I.1.381). This says, in effect, 'Do not become your anti-self.' In a brilliant study, *Inventing the Barbarians* (1989), Edith Hall has shown how fifth-century Athenians, in a gesture which we have come to call 'orientalist', learnt to define themselves by stereotyping foreigners as their own opposites. Athenian dramatists and historians, prompted perhaps by their heroic resistance to Darius and Xerxes, represented to themselves the populations of the 'Asiatic vague immensities' to the North and East of them – especially the Thracians, the Scythians and the Persians – as 'defeated, luxurious, emotional, cruel, and always dangerous' (Hall, p. 99). Every one of these epithets is applicable to Tamora.

Tamora and her sons constitute, after all, the royal family of the Goths; yet their relationship with the pastoral warriors who march through the last two acts of the play is not dramatized. Tamora's name is certainly not Germanic. It is related to the Thracian names of 'Thamyris' or 'Thamyras' and to that of Tomyris, the warrior-queen of the Massagetae – an Asian nation from the unending steppes east of Scythia, whose vengeful ferocity and cunning destroyed the Persian monarch Cyrus. (See Herodotus, *The Histories*, Penguin Classics, translated by Aubrey de Selincourt, 1954, and revised by John Marincola, 1997, pp. 81–4.) As if to reinforce these associations, Tamora is called Semiramis twice: admiringly by her lover Aaron (II.1.22), who, elated by her sudden transformation into the ruler of Rome, confers on her the opulence, prowess and lustfulness of the legendary Queen of Babylon; and as a term of abuse by the chaste and classy Lavinia:

> *Ay, come, Semiramis, nay, barbarous Tamora,*
> *For no name fits thy nature but thy own.*

(II.3.118–19)

Moreover, Tamora is indeed 'very dangerous', not only because of her implacable cruelty, but because that cruelty is linked with what Aaron calls her 'wit' (II.1.10), that is, her virtuosity as an histrionic manipulator. This combination of mimicry and sadism is exhibited by the speech in which she publicly urges Saturninus to 'pardon' the Andronici while privately assuring him that she will 'find a day to massacre them all' (I.1.453). Can this hypocritical eloquence be distinguished from the sincere eloquence of her plea for the life of Alarbus? Or must we conclude that she is a sham, even when she means what she says? But this would be to judge her by Roman standards, which make fidelity to one's word a sacred duty. Her 'wit' is accountable not to truth, but to emotion, in this case maternal passion. In a complete negation of the Roman world of the fathers, she turns motherhood into a form of promiscuity, which knows no scruple of restraint, and reduces her sons to vicious puppets. This maternal appetite even enters into her relations with the admittedly infantile Saturninus, as she demonstrates in her spontaneous nuptial 'contract' with him – her oath that

> *She will a handmaid be to his desires,*
> *A loving nurse, a mother to his youth.*

(I.1.334–5)

It is tempting to conclude that because the Gothic queen and her sons are not anchored in the culture of the Germanic Goths, they are products of 'orientalism', and thus merely melodramatic figures. That, however, would be partially mistaken, for they obviously possess a degree of individual power to which the term 'melodrama' does no justice. Tamora is a deviant Goth imagined out of barbarian elements which include sexual appetite, cunning and arrogance. To be sure, she enters the play as the head of a family, to find herself in collision with the Andronici, whose social reality is not in question. Moreover, her attack on them plainly has that status as its target. She contemptuously deconstructs Roman religious practices ('O cruel, irreligious piety', I.1.133); she is echoed by Chiron's 'Was never Scythia half so barbarous' (134), and by Demetrius's 'Oppose not Scythia to ambitious Rome' (135) – which implies that Roman 'barbarity' so outstrips Scythia's that comparisons are meaningless. That the charge of barbarism is aimed specifically at Titus, licenser of human sacrifices, is shown by Demetrius's derisive identification of Titus with the savage 'Thracian tyrant' Polymestor, killer of the son of the Trojan queen Hecuba, whose revenge Tamora is exhorted to repeat (138–44).

This cultural aggression comes to a climax in Act II with the confrontation of Tamora and Lavinia, who, for a variety of reasons including conflicting ideals of womanly conduct, cannot endure each other. During the hunt celebrating the nuptials of Saturninus and Tamora, Lavinia and Bassianus come upon Tamora as Aaron is taking his leave of her, and turn on her the full weight of Roman sexual contempt, mostly in the form of sarcastic references to the huntress-goddess Diana, salted with racist allusions to the Moor's blackness. They are interrupted by Tamora's sons, whom Tamora incites against Bassianus and, with Bassianus killed, on Lavinia, who is ready for death, but not for what amounts to a gang rape. In the truly harrowing scene that follows, Lavinia's attempts to plead for the values of chastity are systematically counterproductive, only exciting the queen's sadistic appetite, to the point when she has her forcibly silenced and dragged away.

The scene in question also brings out something in Tamora that is more radically disturbing than cultural aggression. It is introduced by two speeches which, as Aaron puts it, place Tamora under the sign of Venus, and himself under that of Saturn – the god of 'blood and revenge' that is 'hammering' (II.3.39) in his head. This mixture opens up a prospect that instantly heightens Tamora's sexual excitement: 'Ah, my sweet Moor, sweeter to me than life!' (51). This excitement continues to rise as the next episode unfolds before her, with her rampant sons, Bassianus's corpse ('his dead trunk pillow to our lust', 130) and the frantic Lavinia; and it reaches a climax with:

> Now will I hence to seek my lovely Moor,
> And let my spleenful sons this trull deflower.
>
> (190–91)

Saturn and Venus have indeed conjoined, but in her.

But this scene's sadism takes an even subtler form. It notoriously contains a pair of contradictory descriptions of a single woodland prospect, first by an amorous Tamora, who depicts for Aaron's benefit the forest glade with its singing birds, its sunlit shadows and the echoing calls of hounds and horns, as a *locus amoenus* (10–29); then, again by Tamora, but now in a murderous mood, who converts it into a Gothic forest of terror and death, into which she claims to have been enticed by Bassianus, and which so works up her sons that they instantly knife him (91–115). This inconsistency of descriptions of the same landscape has generated a number of inconclusive explanations. From the dramatic perspective I am attempting to develop, this second description, with its luxuriating accumulation of *rhetorical* imagery designed to provoke a murder, remembers its erotic predecessor as it transforms it, and acquires an *expressive* layering of sadistic fantasy which an audience, with what is being twice described before them on stage, would be responsive to. A somewhat similar contrapuntal effect is achieved in the next episode, which depicts the entrapment of Martius and Quintus in the hunting pit that already contains Bassianus's freshly killed corpse. Titus's sons are overcome by an 'uncouth' (uncanny, 211) lassitude that may seem no more than a convenience to get them into the pit. In the real time of performance, however, we cannot forget that this strange affliction settles on them at the very moment their sister is being raped and dismembered off stage. The sinister double effect once again focuses on a description. Quintus asks Martius who has just fallen into the pit:

> *What subtle hole is this,*
> *Whose mouth is covered with rude-growing briers,*
> *Upon whose leaves are drops of new-shed blood*
> *As fresh as morning dew distilled on flowers?*

> (198–201)

This obviously evokes the fate of the freshly slaughtered Bassianus. But, as others have noticed before me, it cannot at the same time fail to remind us of what is simultaneously happening out there in the wings. It is scarcely surprising if Quintus and Martius have the feeling that they have strayed into some sort of magnetic field of malevolence.

Act II of *Titus Andronicus* enacts scenes of torture and carnage muffled in woods as deep as the Katyn forests of eastern Poland. It therefore invites readings in terms of metaphysical or xenophobic evil. But Shakespeare also seems to be asking for something less. In creating his 'barbaric' Goths, he makes a virtue of necessity by exploiting the fact that the concept of barbarism is devoid of social content. What these Goths have revealed about themselves is not that they are possessed by satanic powers, but that they are as it were socially moronic. I have argued that the Romans are Romans by virtue of the fact that they have internalized Rome; at an elementary level, the Germanic Goths, too, are shown to have assimilated the qualities of a real if unsophisticated culture. In contrast, these 'barbaric' Goths do not seem to have properly internalized anything, not even Thrace or Scythia. They possess the trappings of a culture, which include the unabsorbed basics of a grammar-school education (IV.2.22–5); they have ferocious maternal–filial affections; but essentially they remain morally incomplete. It is for this reason that they regard the massively integrated Andronici as their pre-ordained foes, and that they pursue them with a visceral as well as an avenging fury.

VI

The one figure of the play who seems entirely to have evaded emotional dependence on others is Aaron. To be sure, he is a Moor (his name is a variant of 'Haroun'), but one that has no more than a nominal connection with the Muslim world. His literary forebears are less the fiendish villain of Peele's *Alcazar*, Muly Mahomet, or the truly monstrous eponymous hero of Greene's *Selimus*, than Marlowe's atheistical Jew, Barrabas, but without even a religion to deride, or a daughter to kill, or an audience to cajole and conspire with. Indeed, in creating Aaron, Shakespeare exploits the strongest theatrical techniques to project an impression of complete autonomy. Because of his colour and stance, Aaron remains extremely visible throughout Act I, but he also remains completely silent. Once the play's great expository scene is over, however, he steps forward and virtually explodes into his soliloquy. This speech, incandescent with the possibilities of Tamora's elevation, is less a tribute to her than to himself. In a mere twenty-four lines, Aaron imprints himself on our perceptions as a resourceful, virile, ruthless and self-exhilarating nihilist. Yet the more we see of him and his exuberant self-delight, the more baffling he becomes. Every moment of his life represents a nullification of those collaborations that build up and preserve human communities. Aaron keeps up a continuous fusillade of self-assertive acts that appear to be wholly self-referential. What matters to him is the perception of his victims' humiliation or pain, rather than the knowledge that he is the cause of it. This holds of his most trivial as of his most destructive performances. At one extreme, his encounters with Tamora's sons are peppered with taunts and sarcasms which they are too dense to register (II.1 and IV.2). At the other extreme, the most cynical of the few actions he performs without intermediaries – the chopping off of Titus's hand at Titus's own request to save the lives of his already executed sons, whom Aaron himself has framed for the murder of Bassianus – may well be the most monstrous practical joke in the history of theatre. But here too my point is that the perpetrator of the 'joke' does not require its victim to know the identity of his tormentor in order to relish its effects (III.1.201–4, V.1.111–20). The Messenger that returns Titus's hand to him blames Saturninus and his entourage; nor does Titus ever learn the contents of Aaron's eventual 'confession' to Lucius (V.1). Aaron's reticence may seem perverse, but it is not incoherent. To seek to be known for the virtuosity of one's criminal invention is to acknowledge the need for applause, that is to say, to accept dependency. At the same time, such autonomy is a perversion that needs constant reassurance that dependent beings are self-deceived. Aaron's preference is for acting through agents like Tamora (who is never more than a mirror for his exploits), and Demetrius and Chiron (who are merely his butts) in the destruction of Bassianus and of Lavinia, and even at second hand through Saturninus in the inculpation and execution of Martius and Quintus. His relish of the role of invisible power behind far-reaching interlocking plots seems to satisfy his deepest needs. He may be a virtuoso performer of villainies, but it is the pain of others that is the oxygen of his life.

In his contemptuous self-sufficiency Aaron claims to be the author of himself. But within the context of this play, his nullification of social reciprocity cannot be taken as a mere given. There is clearly something obsessive about his general aggressiveness – and in particular about his persecution of the Andronici – which, I repeat, cannot be explained in terms of a commitment to Tamora founded on her appetite for *him*, and which excludes taking her into his confidence. He comes close to acknowledging this himself when he tells her, in response to a blatant sexual invitation: 'Blood and revenge are hammering in my head' (II.3.39). Like Tamora, what he cannot bear about the Andronici is their tradition of rectitude and cultural distinction. Although he, and perhaps Shakespeare, are not yet capable of Iago's awesome justification for killing Cassio ('He has a daily beauty in his life | That makes me ugly', *Othello*, V.1.19–20), his need to humiliate as well as torment them suggests that the claim to self-authorship entails what we have learnt to call *repression* – what is repressed being the social self whose inevitable 'return' must be accompanied by the usual symptoms of psychic damage.

Only by invoking what might be called 'the social unconscious' can we begin to account not merely for Aaron's persecution of the Andronici, but also for the famous *volte face* of Act IV, scene 2. I refer, of course, to Aaron's unconditional acknowledgement of the 'coal-black' son (98) that his imperial mistress has just begotten and sent to him for instant extermination. The moment he sees the colour that identifies the child as his own, his acknowledgement of it overrides all other obligations: 'My mistress is my mistress, this myself' (106). He discards at once the political programme, such as it is, that he has based on Tamora. In its place, with equal abruptness, arises a new but no less ruthless agenda: the survival of his son. For what the child has done is to convert his father's black skin from a badge of defiant self-sufficiency into a social bond. Indeed, it has turned him inside out, for the social self, until then buried within him, is now in front of him, smiling back at him (119), forcing him into the role of a father who puts down the Gothic brothers' racial threats – Demetrius's 'I'll broach the tadpole on my rapier's point' (84) – with the truly ferocious: 'Sooner this sword shall plough thy bowels up!' (86). Aaron has been struck by a bolt of 'parentage' (to use the term repudiated by Marlowe's Tamburlaine); but if this bolt deprives him of his survivor's flair, it also alerts him to the danger of seeking refuge with a Gothic army now under Lucius's command. After the double murder of the Nurse (144) and the Midwife (166), and the cradle-switching required for the infant's survival (152–60), Aaron is left alone with him:

> *I'll make you feed on berries and on roots,*
> *And feed on curds and whey, and suck the goat,*

> *And cabin in a cave, and bring you up*
> *To be a warrior and command a camp.*   (176–9)

The protective paternal voice marks Aaron's release into family feeling, but also into the culture, if not the comradeship, of those military pastoralists we have identified as the German Goths. The irony, of course, is that it is this 'humanization' of Aaron that drives him headlong into the hands of the one man who has the power, as well as the cause, to destroy him. Aaron may have acquired a future, but as he shall shortly discover, he has not thereby lost his past.

When Lucius captures him, Aaron is no longer the self-created plotter who might, like his successor Iago, have sworn:

> *Demand me nothing; what you know you know;*
> *From this time forth I never will speak word.*
> *(Othello,* V.2.304–5)

On the contrary, Aaron now spills the beans, and continues to do so as long as he has breath in his body. Has he taken leave of his 'character' of radical independence? It seems to me that his acknowledgement of his child has brought to the surface what before had remained quite unperceived: the contradictions inherent in his stance of autonomy. As soon as he sees who commands the Goths, he knows the game is up; but since, as he has told us, his son is an extension of himself into futurity, that will not matter so long as the child survives. What he has to offer Lucius in exchange for his child's life is the revelation of his part in the destruction of the Andronici. The reason why Lucius is not only ready but eager to accept this deal is that, were the story of the death of his two brothers and his brother-in-law and of the martyrdom of his father and sister to remain suppressed, he would not be able to ensure, as the patrilineal survivor, their rightful place in the ancestral annals. Aaron achieves the survival of his son, but to do so he has to pay the price of consistency. As a 'misbeliever' (see V.3.142) or atheist, he is obliged to rely on the piety that guarantees Lucius's word. Lucius questions the logic of Aaron's request: how can he put his trust in what he despises? But Aaron sees at once that what counts is not *his* word, but Lucius's (V.1.70–85). However, all this does is to relocate the contradiction. Aaron is a metaphysical utilitarian: the value of anything is its usefulness for himself; but Lucius's oath can only be of use to him if Lucius holds it absolutely, that is to say, on grounds that rule out usefulness.

Thus the contract Aaron forces on Lucius ensures his own defeat, and in two ways. On the one hand, it condemns him to a *confession of impenitence* that, once Lucius has been told what he needs to know (87–120), can only repeat itself with increasing vacuousness, as Aaron's replaying of the gramophone record of Barrabas's catalogue of transgressions ('Set fire to barns and haystacks in the night' etc., V.1.124–44) from the *Jew of Malta* indicates. On the other hand, the survival of Aaron's infant son, depending on the integrity of Lucius's oath, guarantees the survival of those values which Aaron is now condemned mechanically to repudiate. And indeed, this effect is subtly enhanced by Marcus's presentation of the boy to the Roman population, as the play concludes, with the biblical 'Behold the child' (V.3.118, cf. Luke 2:34) perceptible only to Shakespeare's audience, not Marcus's, of course, but not the less symbolically redemptive for that.

VII

The intelligibility of a culture presupposes normal states of mind and body. Any radical abnormality, such as dismemberment, puts human beings out of synchronization with their common life. As we have noted, language is defamiliarized by the loss of hands. Marcus, for example, chiding Titus for his extravagant laments over his daughter, warns him not to drive her to lay 'violent hands upon her tender life'; Titus retorts that this is crazy talk:

> *Why, Marcus, no man should be mad but I.*
> *What violent hands can she lay on her life?*
>
> (III.2.22–5)

Ready-made phrases, unnoticed in daily life, suddenly rear up against their users when that life ceases to be daily. In *Titus Andronicus* such disruptions can take subtle forms. Lavinia's fate is the result of a decision by Aaron, 'Chief architect and plotter of these woes' (V.3.121), to convert a sensational tale by Ovid into a real-life scenario – in other words, to produce a strictly crazy confusion of categories.

Most readers and playgoers recognize that Act III, scene 1, in which Titus as a Roman father is exposed to a succession of Aaron-devised hammer-blows – the sentencing to death of two of his sons, the perpetual banishment of a third, the wrecking of his daughter, the vain act of self-mutilation to reprieve his two sons – represents a high point in the early Shakespeare's representation of suffering. Scholars such as Wolfgang Clemen, who studied the conventions of the pre-Shakespearean set-speech lament (see *English Tragedy before Shakespeare*, 1955) have provided us with a yardstick for measuring Shakespeare's achievement in transforming what might have been three hundred lines of formal complaint into perhaps the most intense *enactment* of grief in Elizabethan drama. Every new development ratchets up yet further Titus's psychological anguish, until his moral resistance finally breaks. Although this great scene has to my knowledge not been analysed in detail, its merits challenge the art of the greatest of actors. What is relevant to my argument, however, is its role in the play's structure of meanings.

What the scene offers is a murderous attack on the central pillar of the Roman patrilineal family. This assault on the father is not principally aimed at severing familial attachments, although it certainly tries to do so. Its essential target is what connects that family to the city. Its campaign against the Andronici is an attempt, as it were, to take *romanitas* out of Rome. To what extent this is consciously calculated is unnecessary to determine: Act II has shown Aaron to be a master-plotter; yet Act IV has also revealed him to possess the defining characteristic of the Shakespearean villain: intellect in the service of unexamined feeling. It may not therefore be possible to disentangle the mix of reason and obsession in him. As far as Titus, his principal victim, is concerned, however, there can be little doubt that what the scene of his agony delivers is a man in whom the need for vengeance takes the form of mental derangement.

An intense experience of grief constitutes a social abnormality. Marcus, who is always in full possession of the norms of rationality, finds Titus's outbursts of anguish difficult to take. In the brief respite provided by Aaron's cynical deal (the father's hand for the sons' lives) Titus, who now shares Lavinia's mutilation, threatens to 'breathe the welkin dim | And stain the sun with fog' – the fog of their sighs – if heaven does not respond to their prayers (III.1.210–11). Marcus reproves him:

> *O brother, speak with possibility . . .*
> *But yet let reason govern thy lament*   (213–17)

– to which Titus retorts:

> *If there were reason for these miseries,*
> *Then into limits could I bind my woes.*   (217–19)

But since there are none, the use of outrageous hyperboles is appropriate, even natural: he and Lavinia must respond to each other as the earth to a deluge or the sea to a tempest (218–30).

Titus's extremity of sorrow also possesses a political dimension. The scene under examination opens with his pleas for a reprieve of his 'condemnèd sons'. This is represented by a scenario or tableau – Titus face-down imploring the earth for pity while the Roman judges pass over the stage with the two prisoners 'to the place of execution' – which enacts the gap that has opened up between Titus and Rome. Soon afterwards, he tells the banished Lucius that the city is 'a wilderness of tigers' (54), that is to say, the very essence of banishment itself. Thereupon Marcus enters with Lavinia. The horror of her condition draws out of Titus a response in which the paternal and the political fuse:

> *Give me a sword, I'll chop off my hands too:*
> *For they have fought for Rome, and all in vain.*
>
> (72–3)

The image of the exile's feral 'wilderness' is now no longer adequate to Titus's sense of disorientation; it modulates into the image of a 'castaway' clinging to a rock surrounded by a rising 'wilderness of sea' (94). Aaron's illusory reprieve momentarily revives Titus's collapsing sense of Roman identity:

Good Aaron, give his majesty my hand.
Tell him it was a hand that warded him
From thousand dangers. Bid him bury it. (192–4)

But as we know, the Emperor sends it back, and Titus, even though he cannot help being a Roman, ceases to be one.

The ominously prolonged silence with which Titus receives this final reversal, when even Marcus is forced to invoke 'Etna' and 'hell' (240–41), is something new. He finally breaks it with a yet more ominous burst of laughter, followed by a brief explanation for it that lapses into the predatory 'Then which way shall I find Revenge's cave?' (269). The old hyperboles of grief marking the rising tension between fatherhood and 'romanhood' have gone. Revenge, the supreme barbarian trait, is now in control. Titus can scarcely be said to have chosen his new role; it rises within him in a surge of madness. The scene is almost over, but it reserves a final surprise. It opened with a poignant tableau, and ends with another: the Andronici make a group exit, with Titus carrying the one head, Marcus the other, and Lavinia her father's hand 'between [her] teeth' (281), while Lucius, bound for exile, swears restitution. This is one of the moments which have given this play a bad name. But it is surely possible to perform it, as I think it should be, as a visual representation of a family, though quite literally cut into pieces, refusing to let go, and drifting out of sight still literally holding itself together. The theatrical effect of such visual puns, which are characteristic of the play, may be incongruous, but need not be trivial.

VIII

Aaron's improvement of Ovid's already fearsome tale is etched on Lavinia's living flesh by Tamora and her sons, who have been given a motive by the ritual sacrifice of Alarbus. Aaron, as we have seen, lacks a specific cause. It does not follow, however, that his is a case of motiveless malignancy. As I have argued, he is in a state of generalized aggression produced by a stance of autonomy requiring the repression of the social dimension of the self. Why then does he feel the need to convert his assault on Lavinia into a rewriting of Ovid? It serves no practical purpose: it adds nothing to her physical pain or her moral shame. It may prevent her from communicating her sufferings, but certainly not from putting an end to them herself. If Ovid does nothing for Lavinia, however, he does something for Aaron. By seeking to out-rival the poet in the medium of life rather than art, Aaron adopts before a living woman the posture of the artist before his own handiwork – the product and display of his 'wit'. In short, he aestheticizes Lavinia's suffering in ways undreamt of by Mallarmé or Wilde, in order to express a contempt for human suffering that can only be called satanic.

The imprinting of a fictional character on a living person is certainly pathological. Although Aaron is technically in control of what he is doing – he has a precise intention which is exactly carried out – morally he does not know what he is doing. Plainly, his notion of the human is deficient; less obviously, so is his notion of art. Ovid's fiction is more than a report of imagined events: it is also a *meaningful* report, for even if Ovid is no friend of *romanitas*, his tale shows that Pandion's Athenian family is destroyed by a resurgence in Tereus of Thracian sav-

agery that proves horribly contagious, infecting its two
civilized victims, Philomela and Procne, with an even more
rabid barbarism. That Shakespeare – who could not have
written *King Lear* unless he had written *Titus Andronicus*
first – was fully aware of this is shown by Lear's assertion,
in the play's opening scene, that he is more likely to
welcome the 'barbarous Scythian, | Or he that makes his
generation messes | To gorge his appetite' (I.1.126–8),
than his disinherited daughter. Stories by writers like
Ovid are not merely virtuoso narratives: they are cultural
messages which may explore the limits of civil virtue. In
this perspective, Aaron improves not on Ovid but on
Tereus, and in so doing puts himself at risk, for by neg-
lecting the status of the *Metamorphoses* as a significant
cultural document, he overlooks the fact that as such it
will have found its way into Titus's library, waiting to let
the cat out of the bag.

If, as I am implying, the super-self-possessed Aaron is
a covert paranoiac, how mad is his arch opponent Titus?
(For Titus is indeed Aaron's contrary, since if in Shakespeare's patterning of the action it is Lucius who destroys
Aaron (V.1) and Titus Tamora (V.2), in the patterning of
the *design* Aaron is to Tamora what Titus is to Lucius.)
This question is smudged by the interpolated scene (III.2)
which gives us a seriously disturbed Titus. In the (original)
scene that follows Act III, scene 1, namely Act IV, scene
1, which finds Titus and the remnants of his family in his
house, his general conduct – his handling of his grandson's
fear of his aunt, of Lavinia's impeded attempts to explain
what she is trying to do with her copy of Ovid, and
of Marcus's inspired solution of her difficulties – seems
perfectly rational. But once the terrible truth is disclosed,
Titus suddenly becomes a mysterious figure both to
Marcus and to us. He utters an appeal, in momentous

Latin, '*Magni dominator poli*' (to 'the master of the great heavens', IV.1.80–81), which persuades Marcus that he needs calming. Marcus therefore invites Titus to participate in a formal oath of vengeance. Although Titus does so, he privately suspends collaboration, warning Marcus that he is out of his depth (100), that Tamora remains in power (96–9), and that a long delay must be expected (101–3). Titus decides to send some provocative gifts to the now 'detected' Chiron and Demetrius through his grandson, whose combativeness he seems to reprove (118). Marcus interprets this correction as a sign that Titus is too 'just' for revenge (127), and thenceforth seeks to manage Titus's illness. Marcus has lost touch with Titus's thoughts; but although we can see this, we do not know what Titus is thinking either. Is the threat conveyed by the gifts to Tamora's sons sinister or merely deranged? (Aaron, who spots at once what the sons do not, that they have been identified, regards the gift as a 'conceit' worthy of Tamora's applause (IV.2.30): Shakespeare thus underlines the fact that the arrival of the black infant stops him from warning her against Titus.) Is Titus's archery display (IV.3.50–76) – ostensibly a postal service to the gods above, which, like digging the earth or dragging the seas, is a search for vanished Justice – craziness or camouflage? Marcus and his household, opting for the former, continue to humour Titus's whims; Marcus even redirects, privately, the discharge of the arrows into the Emperor's court (62–3), enraging Saturninus and inadvertently provoking the Clown's execution. (IV.4.45). But what is Titus up to? He highjacks the Clown's petitionary appeal in order to get an extremely threatening message to Saturninus, but in total disregard for the life of his appealing messenger. Is this advertised craziness a cover for an attempt to destabilize the Roman populace, as Saturninus thinks

(IV.4.20)? Or is the very pretence of madness – as it is with another of Titus's inheritors, Hamlet – itself a mark of mental disturbance? Caught between the verdicts of the socialized Marcus, who thinks him mad, and the narcissistic Saturninus, who thinks him sane, we are forced to conclude that he is both. But what this means is not revealed until the long-prepared and overwhelmingly shocking *coup de théâtre* of Act V, scene 2, hot on the heels of scene 1 with its equally unexpected exhibitionistic confession by Aaron.

Until Act IV, scene 2, Aaron and Tamora have been complementary allies. However, the birth of the black child – to Tamora a disgusting as well as a dangerous object, to Aaron the revelation of fatherhood – splits their confederacy, although she does not know it. Even so, their respective fates continue to be structurally related. As we have seen, the autonomous Aaron is turned inside-out by the upsurge of the instinct of paternity; Tamora's power over others, owed to her command of the histrionic and rhetorical arts, converts her into a self-destructive victim. Mistress of virtual reality, she ends by losing her capacity to deal with the real thing.

The consequences of this are shown in the exceptionally sophisticated dramatization of her visit to Titus. That visit is prompted by a political project, which is to use Titus to separate Lucius from the army of advancing Goths. To her, Titus's madness is, as it were, fictional, in that it takes the form of impotent fantasies of revenge. She therefore presents herself to him in the guise of a personified 'Revenge', accompanied by her sons as Revenge's agents, 'Murder' and 'Rapine', who are, of course, what they pretend to be, but who are offered to Titus because 'they take vengeance on such kind of men' (V.2.63). She therefore invites Titus to play his part in the make-believe of her masque. However, in a striking reversal of expectations, failure to distinguish between fact and fiction is shown to be hers, not his. The degree to which, despite or perhaps because of her track-record in *realpolitik*, she is under the spell of wish-fulfilment is probed in the high-wire tension of Shakespeare's dramaturgy, which has Titus again and again tell her to her face that he is 'not mad', and that he knows her 'well enough' (21), that Rape and Murder are extraordinarily 'like the Empress' sons' (64, 84), that she should 'stab them' (47), and – when he is 'assured' that they are personifications – that they should kill themselves (99–103), and indeed that as Revenge she should give the 'queen, attended by a Moor . . . some violent death' because, as he says with a moving simplicity, they 'have been violent to me and mine' (109). Tamora's failure to see what is staring at her in the face, not once but continuously, suggests that it is she, not Titus, who has lost control of her wits.

But this first reversal, dramatic as it is, exists in order to prepare us for a second and this time conclusive one. It takes place in the course of the forty lines during which Titus, with patient explicitness, tells the gagged and bound Demetrius and Chiron – whom he has tricked Tamora into leaving with him – exactly what is going to happen to them, and why. Nothing could be less allegorical than the literalism of this speech, nor starker than the enormity of what it is saying. Titus is preparing to turn his house and its household gods, the source and anchor of Roman piety, into a human abattoir to prepare for a cannibal feast. More generally, he is proposing to convert the social institution of the banquet, traditionally the *convivium* of communal festivity (which Tamora had herself planned to pervert into an entrapment) into an obscene rite of retro-maternity in which 'Like to the earth'

Tamora will be made to 'swallow her own increase' (V.2.190).

Titus's justification of this grotesque design is explicit and assured:

> For worse than Philomel you used my daughter,
> And worse than Procne I will be revenged.   (193–4)

He takes up Ovid's master-narrative exactly at the point at which Aaron left it. In one sense, this is a well-merited implied lesson to Aaron, the incompetent critic, who has taken the part for the whole. But in another, it is an amplification, and not a correction, of Aaron's original aestheticism. Like Aaron, Titus conflates the fictional and the real; but he does so for a very different reason. Aaron's was an expression of solipsistic power, Titus's is a symptom of demented suffering. His aggression, unlike Aaron's, is the reflex of a radical injury to personal identity, which this play regards as relational. Thus it is an injury which legal justice, even when it can intervene – as it emphatically cannot in the Rome of Saturninus and Tamora – is unable to heal. It recalls that self-assertion which Gordon Braden, in his revelatory reading of Seneca's tragedies (*Renaissance Tragedy and the Senecan Tradition: Anger's Privilege*, New Haven, Yale University Press, 1985), finds at the centre of the revenger's madness. Shakespeare, however, makes greater demands than Seneca.

Titus's decision to assume the mantle of Procne is not, as with Aaron's adoption of the role of Tereus, to disregard the meaning of Ovid's tale, but to construct a defiant performance of it. Procne commits what is probably the most barbaric crime in *The Metamorphoses*, an anthology that does not skimp on outrages; but what she does she has been taught to do by Tereus. Titus learns exactly the same lesson from Aaron and Tamora. But unlike Procne, who abandons herself to the luxury of undiluted vengeance, Titus's revenge purposes to be, as I have implied, an affirmation of ancient virtue. At once chef and host to his guests, he presides over his feast as high priest of *romanitas*, beginning with a demonstration for the benefit of the Emperor of Roman tradition at its most intransigent (a re-enactment of Virginius's execution of his daughter), and concluding with the performance of a spectacularly barbaric rite (the killing of a mother filled with the cooked flesh of her own sons). Thus Rome and Scythia co-inhabit Titus as implacably as patience and policy do the mad Lear, who starts his sermon to Gloucester with one exhortation: 'Thou must be patient', in order to cap it, eight lines later, with another: 'Kill, kill, kill, kill, kill kill' (*op. cit.* IV.6.180, 188). With such contradictions, which are defined by morality but which morality cannot unravel, we are brought into the presence of a tragic impasse.

IX

The final movement of the play sees the surviving Andronici persuade the Roman people to elect Marcus to the supreme office on a platform of reconciliation and reconstruction. It then brings the play to a close by segregating the Andronici and the Goths, which it accomplishes by repeating the ritual that opened the play: the burial of the dead. Titus and Lavinia are laid in the family mortuary monument by their grieving survivors, who, though few, represent three generations: Marcus, Lucius and Young Lucius. As for Tamora and the still-living Aaron, they are denied all ceremony and left uninterred under the sky, prey to scavenging birds. This narrative coda is as theatrically skilful as anything preceding it. However, despite the masterly eloquence of the orations, which persuade their audiences because they deserve to, and the structural relevance and clarity with which the corpses delivered by Titus's banquet are distributed, many productions omit, and commentaries neglect or even disregard, these 130 concluding lines.

Among the several reasons for this indifference, which would include the fear of a theatrical anticlimax, one in particular has prevailed over the last two decades: that the reassurance of this moral tidying-up and closing of ranks is a betrayal of the transgressive imagination that has created the play.

For what the play has revealed is not a conflict between outsiders and insiders, but a radical disconnection within Rome itself, a city which indifferently nurtures a Saturninus and a Marcus, and which generates an ideology, embodied in the military Andronici, in which duty and violence are two names for a single thing. The claim is that in *Titus Andronicus* Shakespeare's imagination has opened up and stared into a terrifying reality, but that, as the play winds down, and imagination cools down with it, the normal Shakespearean conservatism takes over, battens down the hatches and looks forward to ever-improving box-office takings.

The assumption behind such a critique is that society, in the sense of civility, collaboration and continuity, is at best a necessary illusion which protects its members from knowledge of the repressions and cruelties which these values entail. Such a view, which may well be as religious or moral as it is political, is not one which I wish to contest. My only point is that it is not relevant to an understanding of plays like *Titus Andronicus*. Such plays are not directly concerned with social diagnosis and reform. Their task is to restore reality to human experience; and this can only be accomplished by the ability to see two things at once. William Blake once noted that no man can understand true art who has not explored and rejected bad art. The reverse is also true: no one will understand the true meaning of violence who does not care for its opposite. To grasp the reality of such phrases as 'barbaric destructiveness' or 'intellectual nihilism', it is necessary to be able to take delight in the playing of a lute (II.4.44–7) or to feel the past alive in the future (V.3.160–65). It is Shakespeare's unconditional commitment to human society that gives his depictions of its disruptions and disintegrations such power.

FURTHER READING

Single-text editions of *Titus Andronicus* currently available include Eugene Waith's Oxford edition (1984) and Alan Hughes's New Cambridge edition (1994). These provide substantial introductions to the stage history and critical reception of the play. Jonathan Bate's edition (1995) in the Third Series of Arden replaces J. C. Maxwell's authoritative but out-dated Arden edition of 1953. Bate distances himself from Maxwell's view that the first act was written by George Peele and that the play is 'much less interesting in itself than as foreshadowing several of Shakespeare's mature tragedies'. Bate persuasively shows that 'not only the play's staging but also its aesthetics and politics are in fact complicated and sophisticated'. Bate is inclined to regard the play not as 'a piece of juvenilia but a new work performed for the first time as a showpiece in January 1594', thus proposing a slightly later date of composition.

Prior to Peter Brook's 1955 Stratford production, which generated new critical and theatrical interest in the play, the reception of *Titus Andronicus* was dominated by the controversial issue of authorship. The most significant contributions to the authorship debate this century range from *Did Shakespeare Write 'Titus Andronicus'?* (London: Watts, 1905), in which J. M. Robertson argues against the hypothesis of Shakespeare's sole authorship, to H. T. Price's *Construction in Shakespeare* (Ann Arbor, Mich.: University of Michigan Press, 1951), which provides internal evidence to support the opposite view.

Critics and editors are now more inclined to focus on

the play's intrinsic merits than on the vexed issue of its origins. Shakespeare's imaginative reworking of his sources, which are reprinted in Geoffrey Bullough's *Narrative and Dramatic Sources of Shakespeare*, vol. VI (London: Routledge, 1966), is explored in Heather James's article 'Cultural Disintegration in *Titus Andronicus*: Mutilating Titus, Virgil, and Rome', in *Themes in Drama* 13 (1991) and her book *Shakespeare's Troy* (Cambridge: Cambridge University Press, 1997), and in Jonathan Bate's, *Shakespeare and Ovid* (Oxford: Clarendon Press, 1993). In her article, James argues that 'Shakespeare first invokes the *Aeneid* as the epic of empire-building, order, and *pietas*, and then allows Ovid's *Metamorphoses* to invade it . . . In [his] treat[ment of] the classical texts of imperial Rome', James continues, 'Shakespeare replicates the tragedy's patterns of competition, mutilation and digestion.' Bate similarly emphasizes Shakespeare's experimental and self-conscious use of his Ovidian source, and argues that *Titus Andronicus* is 'an archetypal Renaissance humanist text in that it is patterned on the classics', and not on an early modern source, as was widely believed. Bate and James, along with Eugene Waith, in his seminal article 'The Metamorphosis of Violence in *Titus Andronicus*', in *Shakespeare Survey* 10 (1957), pp. 39–49, and Ann Thompson, in 'Philomel in *Titus Andronicus* and *Cymbeline*', in *Shakespeare Survey* 31 (1978), pp. 23–32, have amply demonstrated that the influence of Ovid is stronger than any other model and have thus departed from a conventional assumption that *Titus Andronicus* can be best interpreted as belonging to the Senecan tradition of Elizabethan revenge tragedies. See, for example, F. Bowers, *Elizabethan Revenge Tragedy* (Princeton, 1940); Irving Ribner, 'Senecan Beginnings: *Titus Andronicus*, *Richard III*, *Romeo and Juliet*', in *Shakespearian Tragedy* (London, 1960), A. C.

Hamilton, *The Early Shakespeare* (San Marino, Calif., 1967); Nicholas Brooke, *Shakespeare's Early Tragedies* (London, 1968); and G. K. Hunter, *Dramatic Identities and Cultural Tradition* (Liverpool, 1978).

The advent of critical theory has produced a varied range of new readings of the play. In 'Rape and Revenge in *Titus Andronicus*', *English Literary Renaissance* 8 (1978), pp. 159–82, David Willbern applies a psychoanalytic approach in order to demonstrate that the play exemplifies a 'structural reciprocity' between rape and revenge. Alan Sommers's structural analysis in ' "Wilderness of Tigers": Structure and Symbolism in *Titus Andronicus*', in *Essays in Criticism* 10 (1960), pp. 275–89, focuses on Shakespeare's subtle exploration of the binary opposition between the Romans and the Goths. Feminist criticism has also produced interesting essays on the relationship between rape as a literal threat against the female body, and as a metaphorical threat against the body politic. See, for example, R. S. White, *Innocent Victims: Poetic Injustice in Shakespearean Tragedy* (London, 1986) and Catherine R. Stimpson, 'Shakespeare and the Soil of Rape', in *The Woman's Part: Feminist Criticism of Shakespeare*, edited by C. R. S. Lenz, G. Green and C. T. Neely (Urbana, Ill., 1980). The anthropological approach inspired by C. L. Barber and N. Frye, and subsequently qualified by M. Bakhtin and C. Geertz, has also identified the roots of Titus's tragedy with perversions of 'relationships of proximity and conviviality', see Richard Marienstras, *New Perspectives on the Shakespearean World* (Cambridge: Cambridge University Press, 1985) and conflicting ritual observations, see Naomi Conn Liebler, *Shakespeare's Festive Tragedy* (London: Routledge, 1995).

Eugene Waith's article on 'The Metamorphosis of Violence in *Titus Andronicus*' (see above) and his investigation of the relationship between the excess of violence and the highly stylized quality of the play's language has proved to be the most influential contribution to its critical reception. Waith believes that Shakespeare was more interested by Ovid's exploration of the transforming powers of intense passions than by the medieval tradition of *Ovide Moralisé*, but that 'in taking over certain Ovidian forms, [he] takes over part of an Ovidian conception which cannot be fully realised by the techniques of drama'. Although inspired by Waith, A. H. Tricomi rejects the view that 'the play fails to transpose a narrative tale into a convincing dramatic story', and explains instead how its figurative language imitates the literal events of the plot in order to 'keep the excruciating images of mutilation before us even when the visual spectacle is no longer before us' ('The Aesthetics of Mutilation in *Titus Andronicus*', in *Shakespeare Survey* 27 (1974), pp. 11–19). In a slightly earlier and less incisive article, 'The Unspeakable in Pursuit of the Uneatable; Language and Action in *Titus Andronicus*', in *Critical Quarterly* 14 (1972), pp. 320–39, D. J. Palmer develops a similar line of argument to Waith and Tricomi.

The stage history of the play over the last thirty years is covered by A. C. Dessen's *Titus Andronicus*, Shakespeare in Performance Series (Manchester and New York: Manchester University Press, 1989), whereas Gustav Ungerer, 'An Unrecorded Elizabethan Performance of *TA*', in *Shakespeare Survey* 14 (1961), pp.102–9, reveals documentary evidence on a private performance of the play, which took place in the household of Sir John Harington in Rutland on New Year's Day, 1596. Antony Sher and Greg Doran's *Woza Shakespeare: Titus Andronicus in South Africa* (London: Methuen, 1996) provides an entertaining and enlightening account of a production of *Titus Andronicus* staged in South Africa in 1995.

Renewed critical and theatrical interest in the play has prompted collections of essays and casebooks, such as Philip C. Kolin, *Titus Andronicus: Critical Essays* (New York and London: Garland, 1995), Harold Metz, *Shakespeare's Earliest Tragedy: Studies in Titus Andronicus* (Madison, NJ: Fairleigh Dickinson University Press, 1996) and Maurice Charney, *Titus Andronicus*, Harvester New Critical Introductions to Shakespeare (New York and London: Harvester, 1990). Useful introductions to the play can also be found in Dieter Mehl, *Shakespeare's Tragedies: An Introduction* (Cambridge: Cambridge University Press, 1986) and Neil Taylor and Bryan Loughrey, *Shakespeare's Early Tragedies: 'Richard III', 'Titus Andronicus' and 'Romeo and Juliet': A Casebook* (Basingstoke: Macmillan, 1990).

SONIA MASSAI

THE MOST
LAMENTABLE
ROMAN TRAGEDY OF

TITUS ANDRONICUS

THE CHARACTERS IN THE PLAY

SATURNINUS, newly elected Emperor of Rome
BASSIANUS, brother of Saturninus

Titus ANDRONICUS, Roman general
Marcus ANDRONICUS, Roman Tribune, brother of Titus
LUCIUS ⎫
QUINTUS ⎪ sons of Titus Andronicus
MARTIUS ⎬
MUTIUS ⎭
LAVINIA daughter of Titus Andronicus
YOUNG LUCIUS a boy, son of Lucius and grandson to
    Titus Andronicus
SEMPRONIUS ⎫
CAIUS ⎬ kinsmen of Titus Andronicus
VALENTINE ⎭
AEMILIUS a noble Roman

TAMORA Queen of the Goths, afterwards Empress of
    Rome
ALARBUS ⎫
DEMETRIUS ⎬ Tamora's sons
CHIRON ⎭
AARON, a Moor, and Tamora's lover

NURSE
CLOWN
MESSENGER

Senators, Tribunes, Roman Soldiers, Attendants, Goths

Flourish. Enter the tribunes and senators aloft; and I.1
then enter below Saturninus and his followers at one
door, and Bassianus and his followers at the other,
with drums and colours

SATURNINUS

Noble patricians, patrons of my right,
Defend the justice of my cause with arms.
And, countrymen, my loving followers,
Plead my successive title with your swords.
I am his first-born son that was the last
That wore the imperial diadem of Rome;
Then let my father's honours live in me,
Nor wrong mine age with this indignity.

BASSIANUS

Romans, friends, followers, favourers of my right,
If ever Bassianus, Caesar's son,   10
Were gracious in the eyes of royal Rome,
Keep then this passage to the Capitol,
And suffer not dishonour to approach
The Imperial seat, to virtue consecrate,
To justice, continence, and nobility;
But let desert in pure election shine,
And, Romans, fight for freedom in your choice.
     Enter Marcus Andronicus aloft with the crown

MARCUS

Princes that strive by factions and by friends
Ambitiously for rule and empery,
Know that the people of Rome, for whom we stand   20

A special party, have by common voice
In election for the Roman empery
Chosen Andronicus, surnamèd Pius
For many good and great deserts to Rome.
A nobler man, a braver warrior,
Lives not this day within the city walls.
He by the senate is accited home
From weary wars against the barbarous Goths,
That with his sons, a terror to our foes,
30 Hath yoked a nation strong, trained up in arms.
Ten years are spent since first he undertook
This cause of Rome, and chastisèd with arms
Our enemies' pride. Five times he hath returned
Bleeding to Rome, bearing his valiant sons
In coffins from the field, and at this day
To the monument of the Andronici
Done sacrifice of expiation,
And slain the noblest prisoner of the Goths.
And now at last, laden with honour's spoils,
40 Returns the good Andronicus to Rome,
Renownèd Titus, flourishing in arms.
Let us entreat, by honour of his name
Whom worthily you would have now succeed,
And in the Capitol and senate's right
Whom you pretend to honour and adore,
That you withdraw you and abate your strength,
Dismiss your followers, and, as suitors should,
Plead your deserts in peace and humbleness.

SATURNINUS

How fair the tribune speaks to calm my thoughts.

BASSIANUS

50 Marcus Andronicus, so I do affy
In thy uprightness and integrity,
And so I love and honour thee and thine,

Thy noble brother Titus and his sons,
And her to whom my thoughts are humbled all,
Gracious Lavinia, Rome's rich ornament,
That I will here dismiss my loving friends
And to my fortune's and the people's favour
Commit my cause in balance to be weighed.

Exeunt his soldiers; his other followers remain

SATURNINUS

Friends that have been thus forward in my right,
I thank you all and here dismiss you all,   60
And to the love and favour of my country
Commit myself, my person, and the cause.

Exeunt his soldiers; his other followers remain

(*To the tribunes and senators above*)
Rome, be as just and gracious unto me
As I am confident and kind to thee.
Open the gates and let me in.

BASSIANUS

Tribunes, and me, a poor competitor.

Flourish. They go up into the senate house.
Enter a Captain

CAPTAIN

Romans, make way. The good Andronicus,
Patron of virtue, Rome's best champion,
Successful in the battles that he fights,
With honour and with fortune is returned   70
From where he circumscribèd with his sword
And brought to yoke the enemies of Rome.

Sound drums and trumpets. Then enter two of Titus's
sons, Martius and Mutius, then two men bearing a
Coffin covered with black, then two other sons, Lucius
and Quintus, then Titus Andronicus, and then
Tamora, the Queen of Goths, and her three sons,
Alarbus, Chiron and Demetrius, with Aaron the Moor,

*and others as many as can be. Then set down the coffin,
and Titus speaks*

TITUS

Hail, Rome, victorious in thy mourning weeds!
Lo, as the bark that hath discharged his freight
Returns with precious lading to the bay
From whence at first she weighed her anchorage,
Cometh Andronicus, bound with laurel boughs,
To re-salute his country with his tears,
Tears of true joy for his return to Rome.

80 Thou great defender of this Capitol,
Stand gracious to the rites that we intend.
Romans, of five-and-twenty valiant sons,
Half of the number that King Priam had,
Behold the poor remains alive and dead.
These that survive, let Rome reward with love;
These that I bring unto their latest home,
With burial amongst their ancestors.
Here Goths have given me leave to sheathe my sword.
Titus, unkind and careless of thine own,

90 Why suffer'st thou thy sons unburied yet
To hover on the dreadful shore of Styx?
Make way to lay them by their brethren.
        They open the tomb
There greet in silence as the dead are wont,
And sleep in peace, slain in your country's wars.
O sacred receptacle of my joys,
Sweet cell of virtue and nobility,
How many sons hast thou of mine in store
That thou wilt never render to me more!

LUCIUS

Give us the proudest prisoner of the Goths,
100 That we may hew his limbs and on a pile
Ad manes fratrum sacrifice his flesh

72

Before this earthy prison of their bones,
That so the shadows be not unappeased,
Nor we disturbed with prodigies on earth.

TITUS

I give him you, the noblest that survives,
The eldest son of this distressèd queen.

TAMORA (*kneeling*)

Stay, Roman brethren! Gracious conqueror,
Victorious Titus, rue the tears I shed,
A mother's tears in passion for her son;
And if thy sons were ever dear to thee,   110
O, think my son to be as dear to me.
Sufficeth not that we are brought to Rome
To beautify thy triumphs, and return
Captive to thee and to thy Roman yoke,
But must my sons be slaughtered in the streets
For valiant doings in their country's cause?
O, if to fight for king and commonweal
Were piety in thine, it is in these.
Andronicus, stain not thy tomb with blood.
Wilt thou draw near the nature of the gods?   120
Draw near them then in being merciful;
Sweet mercy is nobility's true badge.
Thrice-noble Titus, spare my first-born son.

TITUS

Patient yourself, madam, and pardon me.
These are their brethren whom your Goths beheld
Alive and dead, and for their brethren slain
Religiously they ask a sacrifice.
To this your son is marked, and die he must
T'appease their groaning shadows that are gone.

LUCIUS

Away with him, and make a fire straight,   130
And with our swords upon a pile of wood

73

Let's hew his limbs till they be clean consumed.

Exeunt Titus's sons with Alarbus

TAMORA (*rising*)

O cruel, irreligious piety.

CHIRON

Was never Scythia half so barbarous.

DEMETRIUS

Oppose not Scythia to ambitious Rome.
Alarbus goes to rest and we survive
To tremble under Titus' threat'ning look.
Then, madam, stand resolved; but hope withal
The selfsame gods that armed the Queen of Troy
140   With opportunity of sharp revenge
Upon the Thracian tyrant in his tent
May favour Tamora, the Queen of Goths –
When Goths were Goths, and Tamora was queen –
To quit these bloody wrongs upon her foes.

Enter the sons of Andronicus, with their swords bloody

LUCIUS

See, lord and father, how we have performed
Our Roman rites. Alarbus' limbs are lopped,
And entrails feed the sacrificing fire,
Whose smoke like incense doth perfume the sky.
Remaineth naught but to inter our brethren,
150   And with loud 'larums welcome them to Rome.

TITUS

Let it be so, and let Andronicus
Make this his latest farewell to their souls.

Sound trumpets, and lay the coffin in the tomb

In peace and honour rest you here, my sons;
Rome's readiest champions, repose you here in rest,
Secure from worldly chances and mishaps.
Here lurks no treason, here no envy swells,
Here grow no damnèd drugs, here are no storms,

No noise, but silence and eternal sleep.
>   *Enter Lavinia*
In peace and honour rest you here, my sons.

LAVINIA
In peace and honour live Lord Titus long;   160
My noble lord and father, live in fame.
Lo, at this tomb my tributary tears
I render for my brethren's obsequies,
(*Kneeling*) And at thy feet I kneel with tears of joy
Shed on this earth for thy return to Rome.
O bless me here with thy victorious hand,
Whose fortunes Rome's best citizens applaud.

TITUS
Kind Rome, that hast thus lovingly reserved
The cordial of mine age to glad my heart.
Lavinia live, outlive thy father's days   170
And fame's eternal date for virtue's praise.
>   *Lavinia rises*

MARCUS (*above*)
Long live Lord Titus, my belovèd brother,
Gracious triumpher in the eyes of Rome!

TITUS
Thanks, gentle tribune, noble brother Marcus.

MARCUS
And welcome, nephews, from successful wars,
You that survive, and you that sleep in fame.
Fair lords, your fortunes are alike in all
That in your country's service drew your swords;
But safer triumph is this funeral pomp,
That hath aspired to Solon's happiness   180
And triumphs over chance in honour's bed.
Titus Andronicus, the people of Rome,
Whose friend in justice thou hast ever been,
Send thee by me, their tribune and their trust,

This palliament of white and spotless hue,
And name thee in election for the empire
With these our late-deceasèd emperor's sons.
Be *candidatus* then and put it on,
And help to set a head on headless Rome.

TITUS

190 A better head her glorious body fits
Than his that shakes for age and feebleness.
What should I don this robe and trouble you?
Be chosen with proclamations today,
Tomorrow yield up rule, resign my life,
And set abroad new business for you all?
Rome, I have been thy soldier forty years,
And led my country's strength successfully,
And buried one-and-twenty valiant sons
Knighted in field, slain manfully in arms,
200 In right and service of their noble country.
Give me a staff of honour for mine age,
But not a sceptre to control the world.
Upright he held it, lords, that held it last.

MARCUS

Titus, thou shalt obtain and ask the empery.

SATURNINUS (*above*)

Proud and ambitious tribune, canst thou tell?

TITUS

Patience, Prince Saturninus.

SATURNINUS   Romans, do me right!
Patricians, draw your swords and sheathe them not
Till Saturninus be Rome's emperor.
Andronicus, would thou were shipped to hell
210 Rather than rob me of the people's hearts.

LUCIUS

Proud Saturnine, interrupter of the good
That noble-minded Titus means to thee.

TITUS

    Content thee, prince; I will restore to thee
    The people's hearts, and wean them from
        themselves.

BASSIANUS (*above*)

    Andronicus, I do not flatter thee,
    But honour thee, and will do till I die.
    My faction if thou strengthen with thy friends,
    I will most thankful be, and thanks to men
    Of noble minds is honourable meed.

TITUS

    People of Rome and people's tribunes here,   220
    I ask your voices and your suffrages.
    Will ye bestow them friendly on Andronicus?

TRIBUNES (*above*)

    To gratify the good Andronicus
    And gratulate his safe return to Rome,
    The people will accept whom he admits.

TITUS

    Tribunes, I thank you, and this suit I make,
    That you create our emperor's eldest son,
    Lord Saturnine, whose virtues will, I hope,
    Reflect on Rome as Titan's rays on earth,
    And ripen justice in this commonweal.   230
    Then if you will elect by my advice,
    Crown him and say, 'Long live our emperor!'

MARCUS

    With voices and applause of every sort,
    Patricians and plebeians, we create
    Lord Saturninus Rome's great emperor,
    And say, 'Long live our Emperor Saturnine!'
        A long flourish till Marcus, Saturninus, Bassianus,
        tribunes and senators come down.
        Marcus crowns Saturninus

SATURNINUS

    Titus Andronicus, for thy favours done
    To us in our election this day
    I give thee thanks in part of thy deserts,
240   And will with deeds requite thy gentleness.
    And for an onset, Titus, to advance
    Thy name and honourable family,
    Lavinia will I make my empress,
    Rome's royal mistress, mistress of my heart,
    And in the sacred Pantheon her espouse.
    Tell me, Andronicus, doth this motion please thee?

TITUS

    It doth, my worthy lord, and in this match
    I hold me highly honoured of your grace,
    And here in sight of Rome to Saturnine,
250   King and commander of our commonweal,
    The wide world's emperor, do I consecrate
    My sword, my chariot, and my prisoners,
    Presents well worthy Rome's imperious lord.
    Receive them then, the tribute that I owe,
    Mine honour's ensigns humbled at thy feet.

SATURNINUS

    Thanks, noble Titus, father of my life.
    How proud I am of thee and of thy gifts
    Rome shall record, and when I do forget
    The least of these unspeakable deserts,
260   Romans, forget your fealty to me.

TITUS (*to Tamora*)

    Now, madam, are you prisoner to an emperor,
    To him that for your honour and your state
    Will use you nobly and your followers.

SATURNINUS (*aside*)

    A goodly lady, trust me, of the hue
    That I would choose were I to choose anew.

(*To Tamora*)
Clear up, fair queen, that cloudy countenance;
Though chance of war hath wrought this change of
    cheer,
Thou com'st not to be made a scorn in Rome.
Princely shall be thy usage every way.
Rest on my word, and let not discontent   270
Daunt all your hopes. Madam, he comforts you
Can make you greater than the Queen of Goths.
Lavinia, you are not displeased with this?

LAVINIA
Not I, my lord, sith true nobility
Warrants these words in princely courtesy.

SATURNINUS
Thanks, sweet Lavinia. Romans, let us go.
Ransomless here we set our prisoners free;
Proclaim our honours, lords, with trump and drum.
    Flourish

BASSIANUS (*seizing Lavinia*)
Lord Titus, by your leave, this maid is mine.

TITUS
How, sir? Are you in earnest then, my lord?   280

BASSIANUS
Ay, noble Titus, and resolved withal
To do myself this reason and this right.

MARCUS
Suum cuique is our Roman justice;
This prince in justice seizeth but his own.

LUCIUS
And that he will and shall, if Lucius live.
    Exeunt Tamora, Demetrius, Chiron and attendants

TITUS
Traitors, avaunt! Where is the Emperor's guard?
Treason, my lord! Lavinia is surprised.

SATURNINUS
Surprised? By whom?

BASSIANUS   By him that justly may
Bear his betrothed from all the world away.

Exeunt Bassianus and Marcus with Lavinia

MUTIUS
290 Brothers, help to convey her hence away,
And with my sword I'll keep this door safe.

Exeunt Quintus and Martius at one door

TITUS *(to Saturninus)*
Follow, my lord, and I'll soon bring her back.

Exit Saturninus at the other door

MUTIUS
My lord, you pass not here.

TITUS   What, villain boy,
Barr'st me my way in Rome?

He attacks Mutius

MUTIUS   Help, Lucius, help.

Titus kills him

LUCIUS
My lord, you are unjust, and more than so,
In wrongful quarrel you have slain your son.

TITUS
Nor thou, nor he, are any sons of mine;
My sons would never so dishonour me.
Traitor, restore Lavinia to the Emperor.

LUCIUS
300 Dead, if you will, but not to be his wife
That is another's lawful promised love.   *Exit*

*Enter aloft the Emperor with Tamora and her two
sons, and Aaron the Moor*

SATURNINUS
No, Titus, no, the Emperor needs her not,
Nor her, nor thee, nor any of thy stock.

I'll trust by leisure him that mocks me once,
Thee never, nor thy traitorous haughty sons,
Confederates all thus to dishonour me.
Was none in Rome to make a stale
But Saturnine? Full well, Andronicus,
Agree these deeds with that proud brag of thine,
That saidst I begged the empire at thy hands.   310

TITUS
O monstrous! What reproachful words are these?

SATURNINUS
But go thy ways, go give that changing piece
To him that flourished for her with his sword.
A valiant son-in-law thou shalt enjoy,
One fit to bandy with thy lawless sons,
To ruffle in the commonwealth of Rome.

TITUS
These words are razors to my wounded heart.

SATURNINUS
And therefore, lovely Tamora, Queen of Goths,
That like the stately Phoebe 'mongst her nymphs
Dost overshine the gallant'st dames of Rome,   320
If thou be pleased with this my sudden choice,
Behold, I choose thee, Tamora, for my bride,
And will create thee Empress of Rome.
Speak, Queen of Goths, dost thou applaud my choice?
And here I swear by all the Roman gods,
Sith priest and holy water are so near,
And tapers burn so bright, and everything
In readiness for Hymenaeus stand,
I will not re-salute the streets of Rome
Or climb my palace, till from forth this place   330
I lead espoused my bride along with me.

TAMORA
And here in sight of heaven to Rome I swear,

I.1

> If Saturnine advance the Queen of Goths,
> She will a handmaid be to his desires,
> A loving nurse, a mother to his youth.

SATURNINUS

> Ascend, fair queen, Pantheon. Lords, accompany
> Your noble Emperor and his lovely bride,
> Sent by the heavens for Prince Saturnine,
> Whose wisdom hath her fortune conquerèd.
340 There shall we consummate our spousal rites.

Exeunt all but Titus

TITUS

> I am not bid to wait upon this bride.
> Titus, when wert thou wont to walk alone,
> Dishonoured thus and challengèd of wrongs?

> *Enter Marcus and Titus's sons, Lucius, Quintus, and*
> *Martius*

MARCUS

> O Titus, see! O see what thou hast done:
> In a bad quarrel slain a virtuous son.

TITUS

> No, foolish tribune, no. No son of mine,
> Nor thou, nor these, confederates in the deed
> That hath dishonoured all our family,
> Unworthy brother, and unworthy sons.

LUCIUS

350 But let us give him burial as becomes;
> Give Mutius burial with our brethren.

TITUS

> Traitors, away! He rests not in this tomb.
> This monument five hundred years hath stood,
> Which I have sumptuously re-edified.
> Here none but soldiers and Rome's servitors
> Repose in fame; none basely slain in brawls.
> Bury him where you can, he comes not here.

MARCUS

My lord, this is impiety in you.
My nephew Mutius' deeds do plead for him;
He must be buried with his brethren.   360

MARTIUS *and* QUINTUS

And shall, or him we will accompany.

TITUS

'And shall'? What villain was it spake that word?

MARTIUS

He that would vouch it in any place but here.

TITUS

What, would you bury him in my despite?

MARCUS

No, noble Titus, but entreat of thee
To pardon Mutius and to bury him.

TITUS

Marcus, even thou hast struck upon my crest,
And with these boys mine honour thou hast
        wounded.
My foes I do repute you every one,
So trouble me no more, but get you gone.   370

QUINTUS

He is not with himself; let us withdraw.

MARTIUS

Not I, till Mutius' bones be burièd.
        The brother and the sons kneel

MARCUS

Brother, for in that name doth nature plead –

MARTIUS

Father, and in that name doth nature speak –

TITUS

Speak thou no more, if all the rest will speed.

MARCUS

Renownèd Titus, more than half my soul –

LUCIUS

Dear father, soul and substance of us all –

MARCUS

Suffer thy brother Marcus to inter
His noble nephew here in virtue's nest,
380 That died in honour and Lavinia's cause.
Thou art a Roman, be not barbarous.
The Greeks upon advice did bury Ajax
That slew himself, and wise Laertes' son
Did graciously plead for his funerals.
Let not young Mutius then, that was thy joy,
Be barred his entrance here.

TITUS   Rise, Marcus, rise.

  They rise

The dismall'st day is this that e'er I saw,
To be dishonoured by my sons in Rome.
Well, bury him, and bury me the next.

  They put Mutius in the tomb

LUCIUS

390 There lie thy bones, sweet Mutius, with thy friends,
Till we with trophies do adorn thy tomb.

ALL (*kneeling*)

No man shed tears for noble Mutius;
He lives in fame, that died in virtue's cause.

  They rise

       Exeunt all but Marcus and Titus

MARCUS

My lord, to step out of these dreary dumps,
How comes it that the subtle Queen of Goths
Is of a sudden thus advanced in Rome?

TITUS

I know not, Marcus, but I know it is.
Whether by device or no, the heavens can tell.
Is she not then beholden to the man

That brought her for this high good turn so far?   400

MARCUS

Yes, and will nobly him remunerate.

    Flourish.

    Enter the Emperor, Tamora and her two sons, with the
    Moor, at one door. Enter at the other door Bassianus
    and Lavinia, with Lucius, Quintus and Martius

SATURNINUS

So, Bassianus, you have played your prize.

God give you joy, sir, of your gallant bride.

BASSIANUS

And you of yours, my lord. I say no more,

Nor wish no less, and so I take my leave.

SATURNINUS

Traitor, if Rome have law or we have power,

Thou and thy faction shall repent this rape.

BASSIANUS

'Rape' call you it, my lord, to seize my own,

My true betrothèd love, and now my wife?

But let the laws of Rome determine all;   410

Meanwhile am I possessed of that is mine.

SATURNINUS

'Tis good, sir. You are very short with us,

But if we live, we'll be as sharp with you.

BASSIANUS

My lord, what I have done, as best I may

Answer I must, and shall do with my life.

Only thus much I give your grace to know:

By all the duties that I owe to Rome,

This noble gentleman, Lord Titus here,

Is in opinion and in honour wronged,

That in the rescue of Lavinia   420

With his own hand did slay his youngest son

In zeal to you, and highly moved to wrath

To be controlled in that he frankly gave.
Receive him then to favour, Saturnine,
That hath expressed himself in all his deeds
A father and a friend to thee and Rome.

TITUS

Prince Bassianus, leave to plead my deeds.
'Tis thou and those that have dishonoured me.
(*Kneeling*) Rome and the righteous heavens be my
    judge,

430 How I have loved and honoured Saturnine.

TAMORA

My worthy lord, if ever Tamora
Were gracious in those princely eyes of thine,
Then hear me speak indifferently for all,
And at my suit, sweet, pardon what is past.

SATURNINUS

What, madam, be dishonoured openly,
And basely put it up without revenge?

TAMORA

Not so, my lord. The gods of Rome forfend
I should be author to dishonour you.
But on mine honour dare I undertake

440 For good Lord Titus' innocence in all,
Whose fury not dissembled speaks his griefs.
Then at my suit look graciously on him;
Lose not so noble a friend on vain suppose,
Nor with sour looks afflict his gentle heart.
(*Aside to Saturninus*)
My lord, be ruled by me, be won at last,
Dissemble all your griefs and discontents.
You are but newly planted in your throne.
Lest then the people, and patricians too,
Upon a just survey take Titus' part

450 And so supplant you for ingratitude,

86

Which Rome reputes to be a heinous sin,
Yield at entreats, and then let me alone:
I'll find a day to massacre them all,
And raze their faction and their family,
The cruel father and his traitorous sons
To whom I suèd for my dear son's life,
And make them know what 'tis to let a queen
Kneel in the streets and beg for grace in vain.
(*To all*) Come, come, sweet Emperor; come,
    Andronicus.
Take up this good old man, and cheer the heart   460
That dies in tempest of thy angry frown.

SATURNINUS
Rise, Titus, rise; my Empress hath prevailed.

TITUS (*rising*)
I thank your majesty and her, my lord.
These words, these looks, infuse new life in me.

TAMORA
Titus, I am incorporate in Rome,
A Roman now adopted happily,
And must advise the Emperor for his good.
This day all quarrels die, Andronicus;
(*To Saturnine*) And let it be mine honour, good my
    lord,
That I have reconciled your friends and you.   470
For you, Prince Bassianus, I have passed
My word and promise to the Emperor
That you will be more mild and tractable.
And fear not, lords, and you, Lavinia:
By my advice, all humbled on your knees,
You shall ask pardon of his majesty.

    Bassianus, Lavinia, Lucius, Quintus, and Martius
    kneel

LUCIUS

We do, and vow to heaven and to his highness
That what we did was mildly as we might,
Tend'ring our sister's honour and our own.

MARCUS (*kneeling*)

480   That on mine honour here do I protest.

SATURNINUS

Away, and talk not, trouble us no more.

TAMORA

Nay, nay, sweet Emperor, we must all be friends.
The tribune and his nephews kneel for grace;
I will not be denied; sweetheart, look back.

SATURNINUS

Marcus, for thy sake, and thy brother's here,
And at my lovely Tamora's entreats,
I do remit these young men's heinous faults.
Stand up. (*They rise*)
Lavinia, though you left me like a churl,
490   I found a friend, and sure as death I swore
I would not part a bachelor from the priest.
Come, if the Emperor's court can feast two brides,
You are my guest, Lavinia, and your friends.
This day shall be a love-day, Tamora.

TITUS

Tomorrow, an it please your majesty
To hunt the panther and the hart with me,
With horn and hound we'll give your grace *bonjour*.

SATURNINUS

Be it so, Titus, and gramercy too.
    Sound trumpets

                        Exeunt all but Aaron

＊

Aaron is alone on stage

AARON

Now climbeth Tamora Olympus' top,
Safe out of fortune's shot, and sits aloft,
Secure of thunder's crack or lightning flash,
Advanced above pale envy's threat'ning reach.
As when the golden sun salutes the morn
And, having gilt the ocean with his beams,
Gallops the zodiac in his glistering coach
And overlooks the highest-peering hills,
So Tamora.
Upon her wit doth earthly honour wait,   10
And virtue stoops and trembles at her frown.
Then, Aaron, arm thy heart and fit thy thoughts
To mount aloft with thy imperial mistress,
And mount her pitch, whom thou in triumph long
Hast prisoner held, fettered in amorous chains,
And faster bound to Aaron's charming eyes
Than is Prometheus tied to Caucasus.
Away with slavish weeds and servile thoughts!
I will be bright and shine in pearl and gold
To wait upon this new-made Empress.   20
'To wait' said I? – to wanton with this queen,
This goddess, this Semiramis, this nymph,
This siren that will charm Rome's Saturnine,
And see his shipwreck and his commonweal's.
Hollo, what storm is this?

Enter Chiron and Demetrius braving

DEMETRIUS

Chiron, thy years want wit, thy wits wants edge

And manners to intrude where I am graced,
And may, for aught thou knowest, affected be.

CHIRON

Demetrius, thou dost overween in all,
30   And so in this, to bear me down with braves.
'Tis not the difference of a year or two
Makes me less gracious, or thee more fortunate:
I am as able and as fit as thou
To serve and to deserve my mistress' grace,
And that my sword upon thee shall approve,
And plead my passions for Lavinia's love.

AARON (*aside*)

Clubs, clubs! These lovers will not keep the peace.

DEMETRIUS

Why, boy, although our mother, unadvised,
Gave you a dancing-rapier by your side,
40   Are you so desperate grown to threat your friends?
Go to, have your lath glued within your sheath
Till you know better how to handle it.

CHIRON

Meanwhile, sir, with the little skill I have,
Full well shalt thou perceive how much I dare.

DEMETRIUS

Ay, boy, grow ye so brave?
          They draw

AARON   Why, how now, lords?
So near the Emperor's palace dare ye draw,
And maintain such a quarrel openly?
Full well I wot the ground of all this grudge.
I would not for a million of gold
50   The cause were known to them it most concerns,
Nor would your noble mother for much more
Be so dishonoured in the court of Rome.
For shame, put up!

DEMETRIUS   Not I, till I have sheathed
   My rapier in his bosom, and withal
   Thrust those reproachful speeches down his throat,
   That he hath breathed in my dishonour here.

CHIRON
   For that I am prepared and full resolved,
   Foul-spoken coward, that thund'rest with thy
         tongue
   And with thy weapon nothing dar'st perform.

AARON
   Away, I say!   60
   Now, by the gods that warlike Goths adore,
   This petty brabble will undo us all.
   Why, lords, and think you not how dangerous
   It is to jet upon a prince's right?
   What, is Lavinia then become so loose,
   Or Bassianus so degenerate,
   That for her love such quarrels may be broached
   Without controlment, justice, or revenge?
   Young lords, beware; and should the Empress know
   This discord's ground, the music would not please.   70

CHIRON
   I care not, I, knew she and all the world:
   I love Lavinia more than all the world.

DEMETRIUS
   Youngling, learn thou to make some meaner choice:
   Lavinia is thine elder brother's hope.

AARON
   Why, are ye mad? Or know ye not in Rome
   How furious and impatient they be,
   And cannot brook competitors in love?
   I tell you, lords, you do but plot your deaths
   By this device.

CHIRON   Aaron, a thousand deaths

80 Would I propose to achieve her whom I love.

AARON

To achieve her how?

DEMETRIUS   Why makes thou it so strange?

She is a woman, therefore may be wooed;

She is a woman, therefore may be won;

She is Lavinia, therefore must be loved.

What, man, more water glideth by the mill

Than wots the miller of, and easy it is

Of a cut loaf to steal a shive, we know.

Though Bassianus be the Emperor's brother,

Better than he have worn Vulcan's badge.

AARON (*aside*)

90 Ay, and as good as Saturninus may.

DEMETRIUS

Then why should he despair that knows to court it

With words, fair looks, and liberality?

What, hast not thou full often struck a doe

And borne her cleanly by the keeper's nose?

AARON

Why then, it seems some certain snatch or so

Would serve your turns.

CHIRON   Ay, so the turn were served.

DEMETRIUS

Aaron, thou hast hit it.

AARON   Would you had hit it too,

Then should not we be tired with this ado.

Why, hark ye, hark ye, and are you such fools

100 To square for this? Would it offend you then

That both should speed?

CHIRON

Faith, not me.

DEMETRIUS   Nor me, so I were one.

AARON

    For shame, be friends, and join for that you jar.
    'Tis policy and stratagem must do
    That you affect, and so must you resolve
    That what you cannot as you would achieve,
    You must perforce accomplish as you may.
    Take this of me: Lucrece was not more chaste
    Than this Lavinia, Bassianus' love.
    A speedier course than ling'ring languishment   110
    Must we pursue, and I have found the path.
    My lords, a solemn hunting is in hand;
    There will the lovely Roman ladies troop.
    The forest walks are wide and spacious,
    And many unfrequented plots there are,
    Fitted by kind for rape and villainy.
    Single you thither then this dainty doe,
    And strike her home by force, if not by words.
    This way, or not at all, stand you in hope.
    Come, come; our Empress with her sacred wit   120
    To villainy and vengeance consecrate,
    Will we acquaint with all what we intend,
    And she shall file our engines with advice
    That will not suffer you to square yourselves,
    But to your wishes' height advance you both.
    The Emperor's court is like the house of fame,
    The palace full of tongues, of eyes, and ears;
    The woods are ruthless, dreadful, deaf, and dull.
    There speak and strike, brave boys, and take your
        turns;
    There serve your lust, shadowed from heaven's eye,   130
    And revel in Lavinia's treasury.

CHIRON

    Thy counsel, lad, smells of no cowardice.

DEMETRIUS

>*Sit fas aut nefas*, till I find the stream
>To cool this heat, a charm to calm these fits,
>*Per Stygia, per manes vehor.*   *Exeunt*

II.2   *Enter Marcus, Titus Andronicus and his three sons,*
               Lucius, Quintus, and Martius, making a noise with
               hounds and horns

TITUS

>The hunt is up, the morn is bright and grey,
>The fields are fragrant, and the woods are green.
>Uncouple here, and let us make a bay
>And wake the Emperor and his lovely bride,
>And rouse the Prince, and ring a hunter's peal,
>That all the court may echo with the noise.
>Sons, let it be your charge, as it is ours,
>To attend the Emperor's person carefully.
>I have been troubled in my sleep this night,
>But dawning day new comfort hath inspired.

10

>>*Here a cry of hounds and wind horns in a peal;*
>>*then enter Saturninus, Tamora, Bassianus, Lavinia,*
>>*Chiron, Demetrius, and their attendants*

>Many good morrows to your majesty;
>Madam, to you as many and as good.
>I promisèd your grace a hunter's peal.

SATURNINUS

>And you have rung it lustily, my lords,
>Somewhat too early for new-married ladies.

BASSIANUS

>Lavinia, how say you?

LAVINIA   I say no:

>I have been broad awake two hours and more.

94

SATURNINUS

    Come on then, horse and chariots let us have,

    And to our sport. (*To Tamora*) Madam, now shall ye see

    Our Roman hunting.

MARCUS   I have dogs, my lord,   20

    Will rouse the proudest panther in the chase

    And climb the highest promontory top.

TITUS

    And I have horse will follow where the game

    Makes way and run like swallows o'er the plain.

DEMETRIUS (*to Chiron*)

    Chiron, we hunt not, we, with horse nor hound,

    But hope to pluck a dainty doe to ground.   *Exeunt*

       Enter Aaron alone with gold   II.3

AARON

    He that had wit would think that I had none,

    To bury so much gold under a tree

    And never after to inherit it.

    Let him that thinks of me so abjectly

    Know that this gold must coin a stratagem

    Which, cunningly effected, will beget

    A very excellent piece of villainy.

       He hides the gold

    And so repose, sweet gold, for their unrest

    That have their alms out of the Empress' chest.

       Enter Tamora alone to the Moor

TAMORA

    My lovely Aaron, wherefore look'st thou sad,   10

    When everything doth make a gleeful boast?

    The birds chant melody on every bush,

    The snakes lies rollèd in the cheerful sun,

II.3

The green leaves quiver with the cooling wind
And make a chequered shadow on the ground.
Under their sweet shade, Aaron, let us sit,
And whilst the babbling echo mocks the hounds,
Replying shrilly to the well-tuned horns,
As if a double hunt were heard at once,
20 Let us sit down and mark their yellowing noise.
And after conflict such as was supposed
The wand'ring prince and Dido once enjoyed,
When with a happy storm they were surprised
And curtained with a counsel-keeping cave,
We may, each wreathèd in the other's arms,
Our pastimes done, possess a golden slumber,
Whilst hounds and horns and sweet melodious
        birds
Be unto us as is a nurse's song
Of lullaby to bring her babe asleep.

AARON

30 Madam, though Venus govern your desires,
Saturn is dominator over mine.
What signifies my deadly-standing eye,
My silence, and my cloudy melancholy,
My fleece of woolly hair that now uncurls
Even as an adder when she doth unroll
To do some fatal execution?
No, madam, these are no venereal signs.
Vengeance is in my heart, death in my hand,
Blood and revenge are hammering in my head.
40 Hark, Tamora, the empress of my soul,
Which never hopes more heaven than rests in thee,
This is the day of doom for Bassianus.
His Philomel must lose her tongue today;
Thy sons make pillage of her chastity
And wash their hands in Bassianus' blood.

He holds up a letter

Seest thou this letter? Take it up, I pray thee,
And give the King this fatal-plotted scroll.
Now question me no more, we are espied.
Here comes a parcel of our hopeful booty,
Which dreads not yet their lives' destruction.   50

Enter Bassianus and Lavinia

TAMORA

Ah, my sweet Moor, sweeter to me than life!

AARON

No more, great Empress; Bassianus comes.
Be cross with him, and I'll go fetch thy sons
To back thy quarrels, whatsoe'er they be.   *Exit*

BASSIANUS

Who have we here? Rome's royal Empress,
Unfurnished of her well-beseeming troop?
Or is it Dian, habited like her,
Who hath abandonèd her holy groves
To see the general hunting in this forest?

TAMORA

Saucy controller of my private steps,   60
Had I the power that some say Dian had,
Thy temples should be planted presently
With horns, as was Actaeon's, and the hounds
Should drive upon thy new-transformèd limbs,
Unmannerly intruder as thou art.

LAVINIA

Under your patience, gentle Empress,
'Tis thought you have a goodly gift in horning,
And to be doubted that your Moor and you
Are singled forth to try experiments.
Jove shield your husband from his hounds today: 70
'Tis pity they should take him for a stag.

97

BASSIANUS

> Believe me, Queen, your swart Cimmerian
> Doth make your honour of his body's hue,
> Spotted, detested, and abominable.
> Why are you sequestered from all your train,
> Dismounted from your snow-white goodly steed,
> And wandered hither to an obscure plot,
> Accompanied but with a barbarous Moor,
> If foul desire had not conducted you?

LAVINIA

80 > And being intercepted in your sport,
> Great reason that my noble lord be rated
> For sauciness. (*To Bassianus*) I pray you, let us hence,
> And let her joy her raven-coloured love.
> This valley fits the purpose passing well.

BASSIANUS

> The King my brother shall have note of this.

LAVINIA

> Ay, for these slips have made him noted long.
> Good king, to be so mightily abused!

TAMORA

> Why, I have patience to endure all this.
> > *Enter Chiron and Demetrius*

DEMETRIUS

> How now, dear sovereign and our gracious mother,
90 > Why doth your highness look so pale and wan?

TAMORA

> Have I not reason, think you, to look pale?
> These two have 'ticed me hither to this place.
> A barren detested vale, you see it is:
> The trees, though summer, yet forlorn and lean,
> O'ercome with moss and baleful mistletoe;
> Here never shines the sun, here nothing breeds,
> Unless the nightly owl or fatal raven.

And when they showed me this abhorrèd pit,
They told me here at dead time of the night
A thousand fiends, a thousand hissing snakes,   100
Ten thousand swelling toads, as many urchins,
Would make such fearful and confusèd cries
As any mortal body hearing it
Should straight fall mad, or else die suddenly.
No sooner had they told this hellish tale,
But straight they told me they would bind me here
Unto the body of a dismal yew
And leave me to this miserable death.
And then they called me foul adulteress,
Lascivious Goth, and all the bitterest terms   110
That ever ear did hear to such effect.
And had you not by wondrous fortune come,
This vengeance on me had they executed.
Revenge it as you love your mother's life,
Or be ye not henceforth called my children.

DEMETRIUS
    This is a witness that I am thy son.
        He stabs Bassianus

CHIRON
    And this for me, struck home to show my strength.
        He also stabs Bassianus, who dies.
        Tamora threatens Lavinia

LAVINIA
    Ay, come, Semiramis, nay, barbarous Tamora,
    For no name fits thy nature but thy own.

TAMORA
    Give me the poniard. You shall know, my boys,   120
    Your mother's hand shall right your mother's wrong.

DEMETRIUS
    Stay, madam, here is more belongs to her:
    First thrash the corn, then after burn the straw.

This minion stood upon her chastity,
Upon her nuptial vow, her loyalty,
And with that quaint hope braves your mightiness.
And shall she carry this unto her grave?

CHIRON
And if she do, I would I were an eunuch.
Drag hence her husband to some secret hole,
130   And make his dead trunk pillow to our lust.

TAMORA
But when ye have the honey ye desire,
Let not this wasp outlive, us both to sting.

CHIRON
I warrant you, madam, we will make that sure.
Come, mistress, now perforce we will enjoy
That nice-preservèd honesty of yours.

LAVINIA
O Tamora, thou bearest a woman's face –

TAMORA
I will not hear her speak. Away with her!

LAVINIA
Sweet lords, entreat her hear me but a word.

DEMETRIUS (*to Tamora*)
Listen, fair madam, let it be your glory
140   To see her tears, but be your heart to them
As unrelenting flint to drops of rain.

LAVINIA (*to Demetrius*)
When did the tiger's young ones teach the dam?
O, do not learn her wrath. She taught it thee:
The milk thou sucked'st from her did turn to marble,
Even at thy teat thou hadst thy tyranny.
(*To Chiron*) Yet every mother breeds not sons alike:
Do thou entreat her show a woman's pity.

CHIRON
What, wouldst thou have me prove myself a bastard?

LAVINIA

    'Tis true, the raven doth not hatch a lark.
    Yet have I heard – O, could I find it now! –   150
    The lion, moved with pity, did endure
    To have his princely paws pared all away.
    Some say that ravens foster forlorn children
    The whilst their own birds famish in their nests.
    O be to me, though thy hard heart say no,
    Nothing so kind, but something pitiful.

TAMORA

    I know not what it means; away with her!

LAVINIA

    O, let me teach thee for my father's sake,
    That gave thee life when well he might have slain
        thee.
    Be not obdurate, open thy deaf ears.   160

TAMORA

    Hadst thou in person ne'er offended me,
    Even for his sake am I pitiless.
    Remember, boys, I poured forth tears in vain
    To save your brother from the sacrifice,
    But fierce Andronicus would not relent.
    Therefore away with her, and use her as you will:
    The worse to her, the better loved of me.

LAVINIA (*clasping Tamora*)

    O Tamora, be called a gentle queen,
    And with thine own hands kill me in this place,
    For 'tis not life that I have begged so long.   170
    Poor I was slain when Bassianus died.

TAMORA

    What begg'st thou then, fond woman? Let me go!

LAVINIA

    'Tis present death I beg, and one thing more
    That womanhood denies my tongue to tell.

O, keep me from their worse-than-killing lust,
And tumble me into some loathsome pit
Where never man's eye may behold my body.
Do this, and be a charitable murderer.

TAMORA
So should I rob my sweet sons of their fee.
180 No, let them satisfy their lust on thee.

DEMETRIUS (*to Lavinia*)
Away, for thou hast stayed us here too long.

LAVINIA
No grace? No womanhood? Ah, beastly creature,
The blot and enemy to our general name,
Confusion fall –

CHIRON   Nay then, I'll stop your mouth.
         He seizes Lavinia
(*To Demetrius*) Bring thou her husband.
This is the hole where Aaron bid us hide him.
         *Demetrius drags the body of Bassianus into the pit and
         covers the opening*

TAMORA
Farewell, my sons. See that you make her sure.
                Exeunt Chiron and Demetrius with Lavinia
Ne'er let my heart know merry cheer indeed
Till all the Andronici be made away.
190 Now will I hence to seek my lovely Moor,
And let my spleenful sons this trull deflower.   *Exit
         Enter Aaron with two of Titus's sons, Quintus and
         Martius*

AARON
Come on, my lords, the better foot before.
Straight will I bring you to the loathsome pit
Where I espied the panther fast asleep.

QUINTUS
My sight is very dull, whate'er it bodes.

MARTIUS

    And mine, I promise you. Were it not for shame,
    Well could I leave our sport to sleep a while.
       He falls into the pit

QUINTUS

    What, art thou fallen? What subtle hole is this,
    Whose mouth is covered with rude-growing briers,
    Upon whose leaves are drops of new-shed blood   200
    As fresh as morning dew distilled on flowers?
    A very fatal place it seems to me.
    Speak, brother, hast thou hurt thee with the fall?

MARTIUS

    O brother, with the dismall'st object hurt
    That ever eye with sight made heart lament.

AARON (*aside*)

    Now will I fetch the King to find them here,
    That he thereby may have a likely guess
    How these were they that made away his brother. *Exit*

MARTIUS

    Why dost not comfort me and help me out
    From this unhallowed and blood-stainèd hole?   210

QUINTUS

    I am surprisèd with an uncouth fear:
    A chilling sweat o'erruns my trembling joints;
    My heart suspects more than mine eye can see.

MARTIUS

    To prove thou hast a true-divining heart,
    Aaron and thou look down into this den
    And see a fearful sight of blood and death.

QUINTUS

    Aaron is gone, and my compassionate heart
    Will not permit mine eyes once to behold
    The thing whereat it trembles by surmise.
    O tell me who it is, for ne'er till now   220

Was I a child to fear I know not what.

MARTIUS

Lord Bassianus lies berayed in blood
All on a heap, like to a slaughtered lamb,
In this detested, dark, blood-drinking pit.

QUINTUS

If it be dark, how dost thou know 'tis he?

MARTIUS

Upon his bloody finger he doth wear
A precious ring that lightens all this hole,
Which like a taper in some monument
Doth shine upon the dead man's earthy cheeks,
230 And shows the ragged entrails of this pit.
So pale did shine the moon on Pyramus
When he by night lay bathed in maiden blood.
O brother, help me with thy fainting hand –
If fear hath made thee faint, as me it hath –
Out of this fell devouring receptacle,
As hateful as Cocytus' misty mouth.

QUINTUS

Reach me thy hand, that I may help thee out,
Or, wanting strength to do thee so much good,
I may be plucked into the swallowing womb
240 Of this deep pit, poor Bassianus' grave.
I have no strength to pluck thee to the brink –

MARTIUS

Nor I no strength to climb without thy help.

QUINTUS

Thy hand once more; I will not loose again
Till thou art here aloft or I below.
Thou canst not come to me – I come to thee.

  He falls in.
  Enter the Emperor with attendants and Aaron, the
  Moor

SATURNINUS

    Along with me. I'll see what hole is here,
    And what he is that now is leapt into it.
    Say, who art thou that lately didst descend
    Into this gaping hollow of the earth?

MARTIUS

    The unhappy sons of old Andronicus,   250
    Brought hither in a most unlucky hour
    To find thy brother Bassianus dead.

SATURNINUS

    My brother dead? I know thou dost but jest.
    He and his lady both are at the lodge
    Upon the north side of this pleasant chase.
    'Tis not an hour since I left them there.

MARTIUS

    We know not where you left them all alive,
    But, out alas, here have we found him dead.

       Enter Tamora, Titus Andronicus, and Lucius

TAMORA

    Where is my lord the King?

SATURNINUS

    Here, Tamora, though grieved with killing grief.   260

TAMORA

    Where is thy brother Bassianus?

SATURNINUS

    Now to the bottom dost thou search my wound:
    Poor Bassianus here lies murderèd.

TAMORA

    Then all too late I bring this fatal writ,
    The complot of this timeless tragedy,
    And wonder greatly that man's face can fold
    In pleasing smiles such murderous tyranny.

       She gives Saturninus a letter

SATURNINUS (*reads*)
> *And if we miss to meet him handsomely,*
> *Sweet huntsman – Bassianus 'tis we mean –*
> 270 *Do thou so much as dig the grave for him.*
> *Thou know'st our meaning. Look for thy reward*
> *Among the nettles at the elder tree*
> *Which overshades the mouth of that same pit*
> *Where we decreed to bury Bassianus.*
> *Do this and purchase us thy lasting friends.*
> O Tamora, was ever heard the like?
> This is the pit, and this the elder tree.
> Look, sirs, if you can find the huntsman out
> That should have murdered Bassianus here.

AARON
> 280 My gracious lord, here is the bag of gold.

SATURNINUS (*to Titus*)
> Two of thy whelps, fell curs of bloody kind,
> Have here bereft my brother of his life.
> Sirs, drag them from the pit unto the prison.
> There let them bide until we have devised
> Some never-heard-of torturing pain for them.
>> *Attendants pull Quintus, Martius, and Bassianus's*
>> *body from the pit*

TAMORA
> What are they in this pit? O wondrous thing!
> How easily murder is discoverèd.

TITUS (*kneeling*)
> High Emperor, upon my feeble knee
> I beg this boon, with tears not lightly shed,
> 290 That this fell fault of my accursèd sons –
> Accursèd if the faults be proved in them –

SATURNINUS
> If it be proved? You see it is apparent.
> Who found this letter? Tamora, was it you?

TAMORA

  Andronicus himself did take it up.

TITUS

  I did, my lord; yet let me be their bail,
  For by my fathers' reverend tomb I vow
  They shall be ready at your highness' will
  To answer their suspicion with their lives.

SATURNINUS

  Thou shalt not bail them. See thou follow me.
     Titus rises
  Some bring the murdered body, some the murderers.   300
  Let them not speak a word, the guilt is plain;
  For, by my soul, were there worse end than death,
  That end upon them should be executed.   *Exit*

TAMORA

  Andronicus, I will entreat the King;
  Fear not thy sons, they shall do well enough.

TITUS

  Come, Lucius, come; stay not to talk with them.
     Exeunt with Martius and Quintus under guard,
       and attendants with the body of Bassianus

     Enter the Empress' sons, Chiron and Demetrius, with II.4
     Lavinia, her hands cut off, and her tongue cut out,
     and ravished

DEMETRIUS

  So now go tell, and if thy tongue can speak,
  Who 'twas that cut thy tongue and ravished thee.

CHIRON

  Write down thy mind, bewray thy meaning so,
  And if thy stumps will let thee play the scribe.

DEMETRIUS

  See how with signs and tokens she can scrawl.

II.4

CHIRON (*to Lavinia*)

    Go home, call for sweet water, wash thy hands.

DEMETRIUS

    She hath no tongue to call, nor hands to wash,
    And so let's leave her to her silent walks.

CHIRON

    An 'twere my cause, I should go hang myself.

DEMETRIUS

10   If thou hadst hands to help thee knit the cord.

                  Exeunt Chiron and Demetrius
        Wind horns. Enter Marcus from hunting to Lavinia

MARCUS

    Who is this? My niece, that flies away so fast?
    Cousin, a word. Where is your husband?
    If I do dream, would all my wealth would wake me;
    If I do wake, some planet strike me down
    That I may slumber an eternal sleep.
    Speak, gentle niece, what stern ungentle hands
    Hath lopped and hewed and made thy body bare
    Of her two branches, those sweet ornaments,
    Whose circling shadows kings have sought to sleep
       in,

20   And might not gain so great a happiness
    As half thy love? Why dost not speak to me?
    Alas, a crimson river of warm blood,
    Like to a babbling fountain stirred with wind,
    Doth rise and fall between thy rosèd lips,
    Coming and going with thy honey breath.
    But sure some Tereus hath deflowered thee,
    And, lest thou shouldst detect him, cut thy tongue.
    Ah, now thou turn'st away thy face for shame,
    And notwithstanding all this loss of blood,

30   As from a conduit with three issuing spouts,
    Yet do thy cheeks look red as Titan's face

Blushing to be encountered with a cloud.
Shall I speak for thee? Shall I say 'tis so?
O that I knew thy heart, and knew the beast,
That I might rail at him to ease my mind!
Sorrow concealèd, like an oven stopped,
Doth burn the heart to cinders where it is.
Fair Philomela, why she but lost her tongue
And in a tedious sampler sewed her mind;
But, lovely niece, that mean is cut from thee.   40
A craftier Tereus, cousin, hast thou met,
And he hath cut those pretty fingers off
That could have better sewed than Philomel.
O, had the monster seen those lily hands
Tremble like aspen leaves upon a lute
And make the silken strings delight to kiss them,
He would not then have touched them for his life.
Or had he heard the heavenly harmony
Which that sweet tongue hath made,
He would have dropped his knife and fell asleep,   50
As Cerberus at the Thracian poet's feet.
Come, let us go and make thy father blind,
For such a sight will blind a father's eye.
One hour's storm will drown the fragrant meads;
What will whole months of tears thy father's eyes?
Do not draw back, for we will mourn with thee.
O, could our mourning ease thy misery.   *Exeunt*

＊

Enter the tribunes as judges and senators with Titus's   III.1
*two sons, Martius and Quintus, bound, passing over
the stage to the place of execution, and Titus going
before, pleading*

III.1

TITUS

Hear me, grave fathers; noble tribunes, stay!
For pity of mine age, whose youth was spent
In dangerous wars whilst you securely slept,
For all my blood in Rome's great quarrel shed,
For all the frosty nights that I have watched,
And for these bitter tears which now you see
Filling the agèd wrinkles in my cheeks,
Be pitiful to my condemnèd sons,
Whose souls are not corrupted as 'tis thought.

10   For two-and-twenty sons I never wept
Because they died in honour's lofty bed;

> *Andronicus lieth down, and the judges and others pass
> by him*

For these two, tribunes, in the dust I write
My heart's deep languor and my soul's sad tears.
Let my tears stanch the earth's dry appetite;
My sons' sweet blood will make it shame and blush.
O earth, I will befriend thee more with rain

> *Exeunt the judges and others with the prisoners*

That shall distil from these two ancient ruins
Than youthful April shall with all his showers.
In summer's drought I'll drop upon thee still,

20   In winter with warm tears I'll melt the snow
And keep eternal springtime on thy face,
So thou refuse to drink my dear sons' blood.

> *Enter Lucius with his weapon drawn*

O reverend tribunes, O gentle agèd men,
Unbind my sons, reverse the doom of death,
And let me say, that never wept before,
My tears are now prevailing orators.

LUCIUS

O noble father, you lament in vain:
The tribunes hear you not, no man is by,

And you recount your sorrows to a stone.

TITUS

Ah Lucius, for thy brothers let me plead.   30

Grave tribunes, once more I entreat of you –

LUCIUS

My gracious lord, no tribune hears you speak.

TITUS

Why, 'tis no matter, man. If they did hear,

They would not mark me; if they did mark,

They would not pity me; yet plead I must,

And bootless unto them.

Therefore I tell my sorrows to the stones,

Who, though they cannot answer my distress,

Yet in some sort they are better than the tribunes,

For that they will not intercept my tale.   40

When I do weep, they humbly at my feet

Receive my tears and seem to weep with me;

And were they but attirèd in grave weeds,

Rome could afford no tribunes like to these.

A stone is soft as wax, tribunes, more hard than stones.

A stone is silent and offendeth not,

And tribunes with their tongues doom men to death.

But wherefore stand'st thou with thy weapon drawn?

LUCIUS

To rescue my two brothers from their death,

For which attempt the judges have pronounced   50

My everlasting doom of banishment.

TITUS (*rising*)

O happy man, they have befriended thee!

Why, foolish Lucius, dost thou not perceive

That Rome is but a wilderness of tigers?

Tigers must prey, and Rome affords no prey

But me and mine; how happy art thou then

From these devourers to be banishèd.

III.1

But who comes with our brother Marcus here?
Enter Marcus with Lavinia

MARCUS
Titus, prepare thy agèd eyes to weep,
60 Or if not so, thy noble heart to break:
I bring consuming sorrow to thine age.

TITUS
Will it consume me? Let me see it then.

MARCUS
This was thy daughter.

TITUS   Why, Marcus, so she is.

LUCIUS (*falling to his knees*) Ay me, this object kills me.

TITUS
Faint-hearted boy, arise and look upon her.
    Lucius arises
Speak, Lavinia, what accursèd hand
Hath made thee handless in thy father's sight?
What fool hath added water to the sea,
Or brought a faggot to bright-burning Troy?
70 My grief was at the height before thou cam'st,
And now like Nilus it disdaineth bounds.
Give me a sword, I'll chop off my hands too:
For they have fought for Rome, and all in vain,
And they have nursed this woe in feeding life;
In bootless prayer have they been held up,
And they have served me to effectless use.
Now all the service I require of them
Is that the one will help to cut the other.
'Tis well, Lavinia, that thou hast no hands,
80 For hands to do Rome service is but vain.

LUCIUS
Speak, gentle sister: who hath martyred thee?

MARCUS
O, that delightful engine of her thoughts,

That blabbed them with such pleasing eloquence,
Is torn from forth that pretty hollow cage,
Where, like a sweet melodious bird, it sung
Sweet varied notes, enchanting every ear.

LUCIUS
O, say thou for her: who hath done this deed?

MARCUS
O, thus I found her, straying in the park,
Seeking to hide herself, as doth the deer
That hath received some unrecuring wound.   90

TITUS
It was my dear, and he that wounded her
Hath hurt me more than had he killed me dead.
For now I stand as one upon a rock
Environed with a wilderness of sea,
Who marks the waxing tide grow wave by wave,
Expecting ever when some envious surge
Will in his brinish bowels swallow him.
This way to death my wretched sons are gone,
Here stands my other son, a banished man,
And here my brother, weeping at my woes;   100
But that which gives my soul the greatest spurn
Is dear Lavinia, dearer than my soul.
Had I but seen thy picture in this plight
It would have madded me: what shall I do,
Now I behold thy lively body so?
Thou hast no hands to wipe away thy tears,
Nor tongue to tell me who hath martyred thee.
Thy husband he is dead, and for his death
Thy brothers are condemned, and dead by this.
Look, Marcus! Ah, son Lucius, look on her!   110
When I did name her brothers, then fresh tears
Stood on her cheeks, as doth the honey-dew
Upon a gathered lily almost witherèd.

III.1

MARCUS

    Perchance she weeps because they killed her husband,
    Perchance because she knows them innocent.

TITUS (*to Lavinia*)

    If they did kill thy husband, then be joyful,
    Because the law hath ta'en revenge on them.
    No, no, they would not do so foul a deed:
    Witness the sorrow that their sister makes.
120   Gentle Lavinia, let me kiss thy lips,
    Or make some sign how I may do thee ease.
    Shall thy good uncle and thy brother Lucius
    And thou and I sit round about some fountain,
    Looking all downwards to behold our cheeks,
    How they are stained like meadows yet not dry
    With miry slime left on them by a flood?
    And in the fountain shall we gaze so long
    Till the fresh taste be taken from that clearness
    And made a brine pit with our bitter tears?
130   Or shall we cut away our hands like thine?
    Or shall we bite our tongues, and in dumb shows
    Pass the remainder of our hateful days?
    What shall we do? Let us that have our tongues
    Plot some device of further misery
    To make us wondered at in time to come.

LUCIUS

    Sweet father, cease your tears, for at your grief
    See how my wretched sister sobs and weeps.

MARCUS

    Patience, dear niece;
    (*handing Titus his handkerchief*)
                     good Titus, dry thine eyes.

TITUS

    Ah Marcus, Marcus, brother, well I wot
140   Thy napkin cannot drink a tear of mine,

For thou, poor man, hast drowned it with thine own.

LUCIUS

Ah, my Lavinia, I will wipe thy cheeks.

TITUS

Mark, Marcus, mark! I understand her signs:
Had she a tongue to speak, now would she say
That to her brother which I said to thee.
His napkin with his true tears all bewet
Can do no service on her sorrowful cheeks.
O, what a sympathy of woe is this,
As far from help as limbo is from bliss.

    Enter Aaron the Moor alone

AARON

Titus Andronicus, my lord the Emperor   150
Sends thee this word: that if thou love thy sons,
Let Marcus, Lucius, or thyself, old Titus,
Or any one of you, chop off your hand
And send it to the King. He for the same
Will send thee hither both thy sons alive,
And that shall be the ransom for their fault.

TITUS

O gracious Emperor, O gentle Aaron!
Did ever raven sing so like a lark
That gives sweet tidings of the sun's uprise?
With all my heart I'll send the Emperor my hand. 160
Good Aaron, wilt thou help to chop it off?

LUCIUS

Stay, father, for that noble hand of thine,
That hath thrown down so many enemies,
Shall not be sent. My hand will serve the turn:
My youth can better spare my blood than you
And therefore mine shall save my brothers' lives.

MARCUS

Which of your hands hath not defended Rome

And reared aloft the bloody battle-axe,
Writing destruction on the enemy's castle?
170 O, none of both but are of high desert.
My hand hath been but idle; let it serve
To ransom my two nephews from their death,
Then have I kept it to a worthy end.

AARON

Nay, come, agree whose hand shall go along,
For fear they die before their pardon come.

MARCUS

My hand shall go.

LUCIUS   By heaven, it shall not go.

TITUS

Sirs, strive no more. Such withered herbs as these
Are meet for plucking up, and therefore mine.

LUCIUS

Sweet father, if I shall be thought thy son,
180 Let me redeem my brothers both from death.

MARCUS

And for our father's sake and mother's care,
Now let me show a brother's love to thee.

TITUS

Agree between you: I will spare my hand.

LUCIUS

Then I'll go fetch an axe.

MARCUS   But I will use the axe.

                                   Exeunt Lucius and Marcus

TITUS

Come hither, Aaron, I'll deceive them both:
Lend me thy hand, and I will give thee mine.

AARON (*aside*)

If that be called deceit, I will be honest,
And never whilst I live deceive men so;
But I'll deceive you in another sort,

116

And that you'll say ere half an hour pass.   190
    He cuts off Titus's left hand.
    Enter Lucius and Marcus again

TITUS

Now stay your strife; what shall be is dispatched.
Good Aaron, give his majesty my hand.
Tell him it was a hand that warded him
From thousand dangers. Bid him bury it;
More hath it merited, that let it have.
As for my sons, say I account of them
As jewels purchased at an easy price,
And yet dear too, because I bought mine own.

AARON

I go, Andronicus, and for thy hand
Look by and by to have thy sons with thee.   200
(*Aside*) Their heads, I mean. O, how this villainy
Doth fat me with the very thoughts of it.
Let fools do good, and fair men call for grace;
Aaron will have his soul black like his face.   *Exit*

TITUS (*kneeling*)

O, here I lift this one hand up to heaven,
And bow this feeble ruin to the earth.
If any power pities wretched tears,
To that I call. (*Lavinia kneels*)
              What, wouldst thou kneel with me?
Do then, dear heart, for heaven shall hear our prayers,
Or with our sighs we'll breathe the welkin dim   210
And stain the sun with fog, as sometime clouds
When they do hug him in their melting bosoms.

MARCUS

O brother, speak with possibility,
And do not break into these deep extremes.

TITUS

Is not my sorrows deep, having no bottom?

Then be my passions bottomless with them.

MARCUS

But yet let reason govern thy lament.

TITUS

If there were reason for these miseries,
Then into limits could I bind my woes.
220 When heaven doth weep, doth not the earth o'erflow?
If the winds rage, doth not the sea wax mad,
Threat'ning the welkin with his big-swoll'n face?
And wilt thou have a reason for this coil?
I am the sea. Hark how her sighs doth blow.
She is the weeping welkin, I the earth;
Then must my sea be movèd with her sighs,
Then must my earth with her continual tears
Become a deluge, overflowed and drowned.
For why my bowels cannot hide her woes,
230 But like a drunkard must I vomit them.
Then give me leave, for losers will have leave
To ease their stomachs with their bitter tongues.

Enter a messenger with two heads and a hand.
Titus and Lavinia rise

MESSENGER

Worthy Andronicus, ill art thou repaid
For that good hand thou sent'st the Emperor.
Here are the heads of thy two noble sons,
And here's thy hand in scorn to thee sent back.
Thy grief their sports, thy resolution mocked,
That woe is me to think upon thy woes
More than remembrance of my father's death.

Exit, after setting down the heads and hand

MARCUS

240 Now let hot Etna cool in Sicily,
And be my heart an ever-burning hell!
These miseries are more than may be borne.

To weep with them that weep doth ease some deal,
But sorrow flouted at is double death.

LUCIUS

Ah, that this sight should make so deep a wound
And yet detested life not shrink thereat!
That ever death should let life bear his name,
Where life hath no more interest but to breathe.

Lavinia kisses Titus

MARCUS

Alas, poor heart, that kiss is comfortless
As frozen water to a starvèd snake.   250

TITUS

When will this fearful slumber have an end?

MARCUS

Now farewell flatt'ry; die Andronicus.
Thou dost not slumber. See thy two sons' heads,
Thy warlike hand, thy mangled daughter here,
Thy other banished son with this dear sight
Struck pale and bloodless, and thy brother, I,
Even like a stony image, cold and numb.
Ah, now no more will I control thy griefs:
Rend off thy silver hair, thy other hand
Gnawing with thy teeth, and be this dismal sight   260
The closing up of our most wretched eyes.
Now is a time to storm. Why art thou still?

TITUS

Ha, ha, ha!

MARCUS

Why dost thou laugh? It fits not with this hour.

TITUS

Why? I have not another tear to shed.
Besides, this sorrow is an enemy
And would usurp upon my wat'ry eyes
And make them blind with tributary tears.

Then which way shall I find Revenge's cave?
270 For these two heads do seem to speak to me,
And threat me I shall never come to bliss
Till all these mischiefs be returned again
Even in their throats that hath committed them.
Come, let me see what task I have to do.
You, heavy people, circle me about,
That I may turn me to each one of you
And swear unto my soul to right your wrongs.
    Marcus, Lucius, and Lavinia surround Titus.
    He pledges them
The vow is made. Come, brother, take a head,
And in this hand the other will I bear;
280 And, Lavinia, thou shalt be employèd:
Bear thou my hand, sweet wench, between thy teeth.
(*To Lucius*) As for thee, boy, go get thee from my
    sight:
Thou art an exile, and thou must not stay.
Hie to the Goths and raise an army there,
And if ye love me, as I think you do,
Let's kiss and part, for we have much to do.
    They kiss.   *Exeunt all but Lucius*

LUCIUS
Farewell, Andronicus, my noble father,
The woefull'st man that ever lived in Rome.
Farewell, proud Rome, till Lucius come again:
290 He loves his pledges dearer than his life.
Farewell, Lavinia, my noble sister:
O, would thou wert as thou tofore hast been!
But now nor Lucius nor Lavinia lives
But in oblivion and hateful griefs.
If Lucius live, he will requite your wrongs,
And make proud Saturnine and his empress
Beg at the gates like Tarquin and his queen.

Now will I to the Goths and raise a power
To be revenged on Rome and Saturnine.   *Exit Lucius*

    A banquet. Enter Titus Andronicus, Marcus, Lavinia, III.2
    and the boy, Young Lucius

TITUS

So, so, now sit, and look you eat no more
Than will preserve just so much strength in us
As will revenge these bitter woes of ours.
    They sit
Marcus, unknit that sorrow-wreathen knot.
Thy niece and I, poor creatures, want our hands
And cannot passionate our tenfold grief
With folded arms. This poor right hand of mine
Is left to tyrannize upon my breast,
Who, when my heart, all mad with misery,
Beats in this hollow prison of my flesh,   10
Then thus (*striking his breast*) I thump it down.
(*To Lavinia*) Thou map of woe, that thus dost talk in
    signs,
When thy poor heart beats with outrageous beating,
Thou canst not strike it thus to make it still.
Wound it with sighing, girl, kill it with groans,
Or get some little knife between thy teeth
And just against thy heart make thou a hole,
That all the tears that thy poor eyes let fall
May run into that sink, and soaking in,
Drown the lamenting fool in sea-salt tears.   20

MARCUS

Fie, brother, fie! Teach her not thus to lay
Such violent hands upon her tender life.

TITUS

How now! Has sorrow made thee dote already?

Why, Marcus, no man should be mad but I.
What violent hands can she lay on her life?
Ah, wherefore dost thou urge the name of hands,
To bid Aeneas tell the tale twice o'er
How Troy was burnt and he made miserable?
O, handle not the theme, to talk of hands,
30   Lest we remember still that we have none.
Fie, fie, how franticly I square my talk,
As if we should forget we had no hands
If Marcus did not name the word of hands.
Come, let's fall to, and, gentle girl, eat this.
Here is no drink? Hark, Marcus, what she says;
I can interpret all her martyred signs:
She says she drinks no other drink but tears,
Brewed with her sorrow, mashed upon her cheeks.
Speechless complainer, I will learn thy thought.
40   In thy dumb action will I be as perfect
As begging hermits in their holy prayers.
Thou shalt not sigh, nor hold thy stumps to
      heaven,
Nor wink, nor nod, nor kneel, nor make a sign,
But I of these will wrest an alphabet,
And by still practice learn to know thy meaning.

YOUNG LUCIUS

Good grandsire, leave these bitter deep laments;
Make my aunt merry with some pleasing tale.

MARCUS

Alas, the tender boy in passion moved
Doth weep to see his grandsire's heaviness.

TITUS

50   Peace, tender sapling, thou art made of tears,
And tears will quickly melt thy life away.

    Marcus strikes the dish with a knife
What dost thou strike at, Marcus, with thy knife?

MARCUS

    At that that I have killed, my lord – a fly.

TITUS

    Out on thee, murderer! Thou kill'st my heart.

    Mine eyes are cloyed with view of tyranny.

    A deed of death done on the innocent

    Becomes not Titus' brother. Get thee gone,

    I see thou art not for my company.

MARCUS

    Alas, my lord, I have but killed a fly.

TITUS

    'But'? How if that fly had a father and mother?   60

    How would he hang his slender gilded wings

    And buzz lamenting doings in the air.

    Poor harmless fly,

    That with his pretty buzzing melody

    Came here to make us merry, and thou hast killed him.

MARCUS

    Pardon me, sir, it was a black ill-favoured fly,

    Like to the Empress' Moor. Therefore I killed him.

TITUS

    O, O, O!

    Then pardon me for reprehending thee,

    For thou hast done a charitable deed.   70

    Give me thy knife. I will insult on him,

    Flattering myself, as if it were the Moor

    Come hither purposely to poison me.

    There's for thyself, and that's for Tamora.

    (*Striking the fly*) Ah, sirrah!

    Yet I think we are not brought so low

    But that between us we can kill a fly

    That comes in likeness of a coal-black Moor.

MARCUS

    Alas, poor man, grief has so wrought on him

80 He takes false shadows for true substances.

TITUS

    Come, take away. Lavinia, go with me;
    I'll to thy closet, and go read with thee
    Sad stories chancèd in the times of old.
    Come, boy, and go with me; thy sight is young
    And thou shalt read when mine begin to dazzle. *Exeunt*

*

IV.1   *Enter Young Lucius and Lavinia running after him,*
            and the boy flies from her with his books under his
            arm.
            Enter Titus and Marcus

YOUNG LUCIUS

    Help, grandsire, help! My aunt Lavinia
    Follows me everywhere, I know not why.
    Good uncle Marcus, see how swift she comes.
    Alas, sweet aunt, I know not what you mean.
        He drops his books

MARCUS

    Stand by me, Lucius; do not fear thine aunt.

TITUS

    She loves thee, boy, too well to do thee harm.

YOUNG LUCIUS

    Ay, when my father was in Rome she did.

MARCUS

    What means my niece Lavinia by these signs?

TITUS

    Fear her not, Lucius; somewhat doth she mean.

MARCUS

10 See, Lucius, see how much she makes of thee:
    Somewhither would she have thee go with her.

Ah, boy, Cornelia never with more care
Read to her sons than she hath read to thee
Sweet poetry and Tully's *Orator*.
Canst thou not guess wherefore she plies thee thus?

YOUNG LUCIUS

My lord, I know not, I, nor can I guess,
Unless some fit or frenzy do possess her;
For I have heard my grandsire say full oft
Extremity of griefs would make men mad,
And I have read that Hecuba of Troy   20
Ran mad for sorrow. That made me to fear,
Although, my lord, I know my noble aunt
Loves me as dear as e'er my mother did,
And would not but in fury fright my youth,
Which made me down to throw my books and fly,
Causeless perhaps. But pardon me, sweet aunt,
And, madam, if my uncle Marcus go,
I will most willingly attend your ladyship.

MARCUS

Lucius, I will.

Lavinia turns over the books dropped by Lucius

TITUS

How now, Lavinia? Marcus, what means this?   30
Some book there is that she desires to see.
Which is it, girl, of these? Open them, boy.
(*To Lavinia*) But thou art deeper read and better
    skilled.
Come and take choice of all my library,
And so beguile thy sorrow, till the heavens
Reveal the damned contriver of this deed.
Why lifts she up her arms in sequence thus?

MARCUS

I think she means that there were more than one
Confederate in the fact. Ay, more there was,

40   Or else to heaven she heaves them for revenge.

TITUS

Lucius, what book is that she tosseth so?

YOUNG LUCIUS

Grandsire, 'tis Ovid's *Metamorphoses*;
My mother gave it me.

MARCUS   For love of her that's gone,
Perhaps she culled it from among the rest.

TITUS

Soft, so busily she turns the leaves.
Help her! What would she find? Lavinia, shall I read?
This is the tragic tale of Philomel,
And treats of Tereus' treason and his rape;
And rape, I fear, was root of thy annoy.

MARCUS

50   See, brother, see: note how she quotes the leaves.

TITUS

Lavinia, wert thou thus surprised, sweet girl?
Ravished and wronged, as Philomela was,
Forced in the ruthless, vast, and gloomy woods?
See, see. Ay, such a place there is where we did hunt –
O, had we never, never hunted there –
Patterned by that the poet here describes,
By nature made for murders and for rapes.

MARCUS

O, why should nature build so foul a den,
Unless the gods delight in tragedies?

TITUS

60   Give signs, sweet girl, for here are none but friends,
What Roman lord it was durst do the deed?
Or slunk not Saturnine, as Tarquin erst,
That left the camp to sin in Lucrece' bed?

MARCUS

Sit down, sweet niece. Brother, sit down by me.

They sit

Apollo, Pallas, Jove or Mercury
Inspire me, that I may this treason find.
My lord, look here; look here, Lavinia.
This sandy plot is plain; guide, if thou canst,
This after me.

> *He writes his name with his staff, and guides it with*
> *feet and mouth*

            I have writ my name
Without the help of any hand at all.   70
Cursed be that heart that forced us to this shift!
Write thou, good niece, and here display at last
What God will have discovered for revenge.
Heaven guide thy pen to print thy sorrows plain,
That we may know the traitors and the truth.

> *She takes the staff in her mouth, and guides it with*
> *her stumps, and writes*

O, do ye read, my lord, what she hath writ?

TITUS

'*Stuprum* – Chiron – Demetrius.'

MARCUS

What, what? The lustful sons of Tamora
Performers of this heinous, bloody deed?

TITUS

Magni dominator poli,   80
Tam lentus audis scelera, tam lentus vides?

MARCUS

O, calm thee, gentle lord, although I know
There is enough written upon this earth
To stir a mutiny in the mildest thoughts,
And arm the minds of infants to exclaims.
My lord, kneel down with me; Lavinia, kneel;
And kneel, sweet boy, the Roman Hector's hope;

> *They kneel*

127

And swear with me – as, with the woeful fere
And father of that chaste dishonoured dame,
90   Lord Junius Brutus swore for Lucrece' rape –
That we will prosecute by good advice
Mortal revenge upon these traitorous Goths,
And see their blood, or die with this reproach.
    They rise

TITUS

'Tis sure enough, and you knew how.
But if you hunt these bear-whelps, then beware:
The dam will wake, and if she wind ye once.
She's with the lion deeply still in league,
And lulls him whilst she playeth on her back,
And, when he sleeps, will she do what she list.
100   You are a young huntsman, Marcus. Let alone,
And come, I will go get a leaf of brass,
And with a gad of steel will write these words,
And lay it by. The angry northern wind
Will blow these sands like Sibyl's leaves abroad,
And where's our lesson then? Boy, what say you?

YOUNG LUCIUS

I say, my lord, that if I were a man
Their mother's bedchamber should not be safe
For these base bondmen to the yoke of Rome.

MARCUS

Ay, that's my boy! Thy father hath full oft
110   For his ungrateful country done the like.

YOUNG LUCIUS

And, uncle, so will I, and if I live.

TITUS

Come, go with me into mine armoury.
Lucius, I'll fit thee, and withal my boy
Shall carry from me to the Empress' sons
Presents that I intend to send them both.

Come, come, thou'lt do my message, wilt thou
    not?
YOUNG LUCIUS
  Ay, with my dagger in their bosoms, grandsire.
TITUS
  No, boy, not so. I'll teach thee another course.
  Lavinia, come. Marcus, look to my house;
  Lucius and I'll go brave it at the court.   120
  Ay, marry, will we, sir, and we'll be waited on.
              Exeunt Titus, Lavinia, and boy

MARCUS
  O heavens, can you hear a good man groan
  And not relent, or not compassion him?
  Marcus, attend him in his ecstasy,
  That hath more scars of sorrow in his heart
  Than foemen's marks upon his battered shield,
  But yet so just that he will not revenge.
  Revenge the heavens for old Andronicus!   *Exit*

    Enter Aaron, Chiron, and Demetrius at one door; and IV.2
    at the other door young Lucius and another with a
    bundle of weapons and verses writ upon them
CHIRON
  Demetrius, here's the son of Lucius;
  He hath some message to deliver us.
AARON
  Ay, some mad message from his mad grandfather.
YOUNG LUCIUS
  My lords, with all the humbleness I may,
  I greet your honours from Andronicus –
  (*Aside*) And pray the Roman gods confound you both.
DEMETRIUS
  Gramercy, lovely Lucius, what's the news?

IV.2

YOUNG LUCIUS (*aside*)

That you are both deciphered, that's the news,
For villains marked with rape. (*To all*) May it please
    you,
10 My grandsire, well advised, hath sent by me
The goodliest weapons of his armoury
To gratify your honourable youth,
The hope of Rome, for so he bid me say.
    Attendants give weapons
And so I do, and with his gifts present
Your lordships, that, whenever you have need,
You may be armèd and appointed well.
And so I leave you both – (*aside*) like bloody villains.
    Exit with attendant

DEMETRIUS

What's here? A scroll, and written round about?
Let's see:
20 '*Integer vitae scelerisque purus,*
  Non eget Mauri iaculis, nec arcu.'

CHIRON

O, 'tis a verse in Horace, I know it well;
I read it in the grammar long ago.

AARON

Ay, just – a verse in Horace, right you have it.
(*Aside*) Now what a thing it is to be an ass!
Here's no sound jest. The old man hath found their
    guilt,
And sends them weapons wrapped about with lines
That wound beyond their feeling to the quick.
But were our witty Empress well afoot,
30 She would applaud Andronicus' conceit.
But let her rest in her unrest awhile.
(*To Chiron and Demetrius*)
And now, young lords, was't not a happy star

Led us to Rome, strangers, and more than so,
Captives, to be advancèd to this height?
It did me good before the palace gate
To brave the tribune in his brother's hearing.

DEMETRIUS

But me more good to see so great a lord
Basely insinuate and send us gifts.

AARON

Had he not reason, Lord Demetrius?
Did you not use his daughter very friendly?   40

DEMETRIUS

I would we had a thousand Roman dames
At such a bay, by turn to serve our lust.

CHIRON

A charitable wish, and full of love.

AARON

Here lacks but your mother for to say amen.

CHIRON

And that would she, for twenty thousand more.

DEMETRIUS

Come, let us go and pray to all the gods
For our belovèd mother in her pains.

AARON (aside)

Pray to the devils; the gods have given us over.
        Trumpets sound

DEMETRIUS

Why do the Emperor's trumpets flourish thus?

CHIRON

Belike for joy the Emperor hath a son.   50

DEMETRIUS

Soft, who comes here?
        Enter Nurse with a blackamoor child

NURSE   Good morrow, lords.
O, tell me, did you see Aaron the Moor?

AARON

Well, more or less, or ne'er a whit at all.

Here Aaron is, and what with Aaron now?

NURSE

O, gentle Aaron, we are all undone.

Now help, or woe betide thee evermore!

AARON

Why, what a caterwauling dost thou keep.

What dost thou wrap and fumble in thy arms?

NURSE

O, that which I would hide from heaven's eye,

60 Our Empress' shame and stately Rome's disgrace:

She is delivered, lords, she is delivered.

AARON

To whom?

NURSE   I mean she is brought abed.

AARON

Well, God give her good rest. What hath he sent her?

NURSE

A devil.

AARON   Why then, she is the devil's dam:

A joyful issue.

NURSE

A joyless, dismal, black, and sorrowful issue.

Here is the babe, as loathsome as a toad

Amongst the fair-faced breeders of our clime.

The Empress sends it thee, thy stamp, thy seal,

70 And bids thee christen it with thy dagger's point.

AARON

Zounds, ye whore, is black so base a hue?

(*To the baby*)

Sweete blowze, you are a beauteous blossom, sure.

DEMETRIUS

Villain, what hast thou done?

AARON

    That which thou canst not undo.

CHIRON

    Thou hast undone our mother.

AARON

    Villain, I have done thy mother.

DEMETRIUS

    And therein, hellish dog, thou hast undone her.
    Woe to her chance, and damned her loathèd choice!
    Accursed the offspring of so foul a fiend!

CHIRON

    It shall not live.

AARON   It shall not die.   80

NURSE

    Aaron, it must, the mother wills it so.

AARON

    What, must it, nurse? Then let no man but I
    Do execution on my flesh and blood.

DEMETRIUS

    I'll broach the tadpole on my rapier's point.
    Nurse, give it me; my sword shall soon dispatch it.

AARON (*taking the child and drawing his sword*)

    Sooner this sword shall plough thy bowels up!
    Stay, murderous villains, will you kill your brother?
    Now, by the burning tapers of the sky
    That shone so brightly when this boy was got,
    He dies upon my scimitar's sharp point   90
    That touches this, my first-born son and heir.
    I tell you, younglings, not Enceladus
    With all his threat'ning band of Typhon's brood,
    Nor great Alcides, nor the god of war,
    Shall seize this prey out of his father's hands.
    What, what, ye sanguine shallow-hearted boys,
    Ye white-limed walls, ye alehouse painted signs!

Coal-black is better than another hue,
In that it scorns to bear another hue:
100 For all the water in the ocean
Can never turn the swan's black legs to white,
Although she lave them hourly in the flood.
(*To Nurse*) Tell the Empress from me I am of age
To keep mine own, excuse it how she can.

DEMETRIUS

Wilt thou betray thy noble mistress thus?

AARON

My mistress is my mistress, this myself,
The vigour and the picture of my youth.
This before all the world do I prefer;
This maugre all the world will I keep safe,
110 Or some of you shall smoke for it in Rome.

DEMETRIUS

By this our mother is for ever shamed.

CHIRON

Rome will despise her for this foul escape.

NURSE

The Emperor in his rage will doom her death.

CHIRON

I blush to think upon this ignomy.

AARON

Why, there's the privilege your beauty bears.
Fie, treacherous hue, that will betray with
      blushing
The close enacts and counsels of thy heart.
Here's a young lad framed of another leer.
Look how the black slave smiles upon the father,
120 As who should say, 'Old lad, I am thine own.'
He is your brother, lords, sensibly fed
Of that self blood that first gave life to you,
And from that womb where you imprisoned were

He is enfranchisèd and come to light.
Nay, he is your brother by the surer side,
Although my seal be stampèd in his face.

NURSE
Aaron, what shall I say unto the Empress?

DEMETRIUS
Advise thee, Aaron, what is to be done,
And we will all subscribe to thy advice.
Save thou the child, so we may all be safe.   130

AARON
Then sit we down and let us all consult.
My son and I will have the wind of you.
Keep there. (*They sit*)
                    Now talk at pleasure of your safety.

DEMETRIUS (*to Nurse*)
How many women saw this child of his?

AARON
Why, so, brave lords, when we join in league
I am a lamb, but if you brave the Moor,
The chafèd boar, the mountain lioness,
The ocean, swells not so as Aaron storms.
(*To Nurse*) But say again, how many saw the child?

NURSE
Cornelia the midwife, and myself,   140
And no one else but the delivered Empress.

AARON
The Empress, the midwife, and yourself.
Two may keep counsel when the third's away.
Go to the Empress, tell her this I said:
    He kills her
'Wheak, wheak!' – so cries a pig prepared to the spit.
    All stand up

DEMETRIUS
What mean'st thou, Aaron? Wherefore didst thou this?

AARON

    O Lord, sir, 'tis a deed of policy.
    Shall she live to betray this guilt of ours?
    A long-tongued, babbling gossip? No, lords, no.
150   And now be it known to you my full intent.
    Not far, one Muly lives, my countryman:
    His wife but yesternight was brought to bed;
    His child is like to her, fair as you are.
    Go pack with him and give the mother gold,
    And tell them both the circumstance of all,
    And how by this their child shall be advanced,
    And be receivèd for the Emperor's heir,
    And substituted in the place of mine
    To calm this tempest whirling in the court,
160   And let the Emperor dandle him for his own.
    Hark ye, lords, (*pointing to the Nurse*)
                      you see I have given her physic,
    And you must needs bestow her funeral.
    The fields are near, and you are gallant grooms.
    This done, see that you take no longer days,
    But send the midwife presently to me.
    The midwife and the Nurse well made away,
    Then let the ladies tattle what they please.

CHIRON

    Aaron, I see thou wilt not trust the air
    With secrets.

DEMETRIUS   For this care of Tamora,
170   Herself and hers are highly bound to thee.
        Exeunt Chiron and Demetrius with the Nurse's body

AARON

    Now to the Goths, as swift as swallow flies,
    There to dispose this treasure in mine arms,
    And secretly to greet the Empress' friends.
    Come on, you thick-lipped slave, I'll bear you hence,

For it is you that puts us to our shifts.
I'll make you feed on berries and on roots,
And feed on curds and whey, and suck the goat,
And cabin in a cave, and bring you up
To be a warrior and command a camp.   *Exit*

Enter Titus, old Marcus, his son Publius, young IV.3
Lucius, and other gentlemen (Caius, Sempronius)
with bows, and Titus bears the arrows with letters on
the ends of them

TITUS

Come, Marcus, come; kinsmen, this is the way.
Sir boy, let me see your archery.
Look ye draw home enough, and 'tis there straight.
Terras Astraea reliquit: be you remembered, Marcus,
She's gone, she's fled. Sirs, take you to your tools.
You, cousins, shall go sound the ocean,
And cast your nets:
Happily you may catch her in the sea,
Yet there's as little justice as at land.
No, Publius and Sempronius, you must do it.   10
'Tis you must dig with mattock and with spade,
And pierce the inmost centre of the earth.
Then, when you come to Pluto's region,
I pray you deliver him this petition.
Tell him it is for justice and for aid,
And that it comes from old Andronicus,
Shaken with sorrows in ungrateful Rome.
Ah, Rome! Well, well, I made thee miserable
What time I threw the people's suffrages
On him that thus doth tyrannize o'er me.   20
Go, get you gone, and pray be careful all,
And leave you not a man-of-war unsearched.

This wicked Emperor may have shipped her hence,
And, kinsmen, then we may go pipe for justice.

MARCUS

O Publius, is not this a heavy case,
To see thy noble uncle thus distract?

PUBLIUS

Therefore, my lords, it highly us concerns
By day and night t'attend him carefully
And feed his humour kindly as we may,
30   Till time beget some careful remedy.

MARCUS

Kinsmen, his sorrows are past remedy.
But [   ]
Join with the Goths, and with revengeful war
Take wreak on Rome for this ingratitude,
And vengeance on the traitor Saturnine.

TITUS

Publius, how now? How now, my masters?
What, have you met with her?

PUBLIUS

No, my good lord, but Pluto sends you word
If you will have Revenge from hell, you shall.
40   Marry, for Justice, she is so employed,
He thinks with Jove in heaven, or somewhere else,
So that perforce you must needs stay a time.

TITUS

He doth me wrong to feed me with delays.
I'll dive into the burning lake below
And pull her out of Acheron by the heels.
Marcus, we are but shrubs, no cedars we,
No big-boned men framed of the Cyclops' size,
But metal, Marcus, steel to the very back,
Yet wrung with wrongs more than our backs can bear.
50   And sith there's no justice in earth nor hell,

We will solicit heaven and move the gods
To send down Justice for to wreak our wrongs.
Come, to this gear. You are a good archer, Marcus.
    He gives them the arrows
'*Ad Jovem*', that's for you. Here, '*Ad Apollinem*';
'*Ad Martem*', that's for myself.
Here, boy, 'To Pallas'. Here, 'To Mercury'.
'To Saturn', Caius, not to Saturnine!
You were as good to shoot against the wind.
To it, boy! Marcus, loose when I bid.
Of my word, I have written to effect: 60
There's not a god left unsolicited.

MARCUS (*aside*)
Kinsmen, shoot all your shafts into the court;
We will afflict the Emperor in his pride.

TITUS
Now, masters, draw. (*They shoot*)
                   O, well said, Lucius!
Good boy, in Virgo's lap! Give it Pallas!

MARCUS
My lord, I aimed a mile beyond the moon:
Your letter is with Jupiter by this.

TITUS
Ha, ha! Publius, Publius, what hast thou done?
See, see, thou hast shot off one of Taurus' horns.

MARCUS
This was the sport, my lord! When Publius shot,   70
The Bull, being galled, gave Aries such a knock
That down fell both the Ram's horns in the court,
And who should find them but the Empress' villain!
She laughed, and told the Moor he should not choose
But give them to his master for a present.

TITUS
Why, there it goes. God give his lordship joy.

IV.3

Enter the Clown with a basket and two pigeons in it
News, news from heaven! Marcus, the post is come.
Sirrah, what tidings? Have you any letters?
Shall I have justice? What says Jupiter?

80 CLOWN Ho, the gibbet-maker? He says that he hath taken
them down again, for the man must not be hanged till
the next week.

TITUS
But what says Jupiter, I ask thee?

CLOWN Alas sir, I know not Jubiter. I never drank with
him in all my life.

TITUS
Why, villain, art not thou the carrier?

CLOWN Ay, of my pigeons, sir, nothing else.

TITUS
Why, didst thou not come from heaven?

CLOWN From heaven? Alas, sir, I never came there. God
90 forbid I should be so bold to press to heaven in my
young days. Why, I am going with my pigeons to the
tribunal plebs to take up a matter of brawl betwixt my
uncle and one of the Emperal's men.

MARCUS (*to Titus*) Why, sir, that is as fit as can be to serve
for your oration, and let him deliver the pigeons to the
Emperor from you.

TITUS Tell me, can you deliver an oration to the Emperor
with a grace?

CLOWN Nay, truly sir, I could never say grace in all my
100 life.

TITUS
Sirrah, come hither; make no more ado,
But give your pigeons to the Emperor.
By me thou shalt have justice at his hands.
Hold, hold. (*Gives him money*)
  Meanwhile, here's money for thy charges.

Give me pen and ink. (*Writes*)
Sirrah, can you with a grace deliver up a supplication?

CLOWN Ay, sir.

TITUS (*gives letter*) Then here is a supplication for you,
and when you come to him, at the first approach you
must kneel, then kiss his foot, then deliver up your   110
pigeons, and then look for your reward. I'll be at hand,
sir; see you do it bravely.

CLOWN I warrant you, sir. Let me alone.

TITUS

Sirrah, hast thou a knife? Come, let me see it.
       Takes a knife and gives it to Marcus
Here, Marcus, fold it in the oration;
(*To the Clown*)
For thou must hold it like an humble suppliant,
And when thou hast given it to the Emperor,
Knock at my door, and tell me what he says.

CLOWN

God be with you sir. I will.   *Exit*

TITUS

Come, Marcus, let us go. Publius, follow me.   *Exeunt*   120

       Enter Emperor and Empress and her two sons, Chiron   IV.4
       and Demetrius, and attendants. The Emperor brings
       the arrows in his hand that Titus shot at him

SATURNINUS

Why, lords, what wrongs are these! Was ever seen
An emperor in Rome thus overborne,
Troubled, confronted thus, and for the extent
Of egall justice, used in such contempt?
My lords, you know, as know the mightful gods,
However these disturbers of our peace
Buzz in the people's ears, there naught hath past

141

But even with law against the wilful sons
Of old Andronicus. And what and if
His sorrows have so overwhelmed his wits?
Shall we be thus afflicted in his wreaks,
His fits, his frenzy, and his bitterness?
And now he writes to heaven for his redress.
See here's 'To Jove', and this 'To Mercury',
This 'To Apollo', this 'To the god of war' –
Sweet scrolls to fly about the streets of Rome!
What's this but libelling against the Senate,
And blazoning our unjustice everywhere?
A goodly humour, is it not, my lords? –
As who would say, in Rome no justice were.
But if I live, his feignèd ecstasies
Shall be no shelter to these outrages,
But he and his shall know that justice lives
In Saturninus' health, whom, if he sleep,
He'll so awake as he in fury shall
Cut off the proud'st conspirator that lives.

TAMORA

My gracious lord, my lovely Saturnine,
Lord of my life, commander of my thoughts,
Calm thee and bear the faults of Titus' age,
Th'effects of sorrow for his valiant sons,
Whose loss hath pierced him deep and scarred his
    heart;
And rather comfort his distressèd plight
Than prosecute the meanest or the best
For these contempts. (*Aside*) Why, thus it shall
    become
High-witted Tamora to gloze with all.
But, Titus, I have touched thee to the quick:
Thy life-blood out, if Aaron now be wise,
Then is all safe, the anchor in the port.

142

Enter Clown

How now, good fellow, wouldst thou speak with us?

CLOWN Yea, forsooth, an your mistress-ship be Emperial. 40

TAMORA Empress I am, but yonder sits the Emperor.

CLOWN 'Tis he. God and Saint Stephen give you good
    e'en. I have brought you a letter and a couple of pigeons
    here.

    Saturninus reads the letter

SATURNINUS (*to attendants*)

Go, take him away and hang him presently.

CLOWN How much money must I have?

TAMORA Come, sirrah, you must be hanged.

CLOWN Hanged, by'Lady? Then I have brought up a neck
    to a fair end.   *Exit guarded*

SATURNINUS

Despiteful and intolerable wrongs!   50

Shall I endure this monstrous villainy?

I know from whence this same device proceeds.

May this be borne? As if his traitorous sons,

That died by law for murder of our brother,

Have by my means been butchered wrongfully.

Go, drag the villain hither by the hair.

Nor age nor honour shall shape privilege.

For this proud mock I'll be thy slaughterman,

Sly, frantic wretch, that holp'st to make me great,

In hope thyself should govern Rome and me.   60

    Enter Aemilius, a messenger

What news with thee, Aemilius?

AEMILIUS

Arm, my lords! Rome never had more cause:

The Goths have gathered head, and with a power

Of high-resolvèd men, bent to the spoil,

They hither march amain, under conduct

Of Lucius, son to old Andronicus,

Who threats in course of this revenge to do
As much as ever Coriolanus did.

SATURNINUS
Is warlike Lucius general of the Goths?
70 These tidings nip me, and I hang the head
As flowers with frost, or grass beat down with storms.
Ay, now begins our sorrows to approach.
'Tis he the common people love so much;
Myself hath often heard them say,
When I have walkèd like a private man,
That Lucius' banishment was wrongfully,
And they have wished that Lucius were their emperor.

TAMORA
Why should you fear? Is not your city strong?

SATURNINUS
Ay, but the citizens favour Lucius,
80 And will revolt from me to succour him.

TAMORA
King, be thy thoughts imperious like thy name.
Is the sun dimmed, that gnats do fly in it?
The eagle suffers little birds to sing,
And is not careful what they mean thereby,
Knowing that with the shadow of his wings
He can at pleasure stint their melody:
Even so mayst thou the giddy men of Rome.
Then cheer thy spirit; for know thou, Emperor,
I will enchant the old Andronicus
90 With words more sweet and yet more dangerous
Than baits to fish, or honey-stalks to sheep,
When as the one is wounded with the bait,
The other rotted with delicious feed.

SATURNINUS
But he will not entreat his son for us.

TAMORA

    If Tamora entreat him, then he will,
    For I can smooth and fill his agèd ears
    With golden promises, that were his heart
    Almost impregnable, his old ears deaf,
    Yet should both ear and heart obey my tongue.
    (*To Aemilius*)
    Go thou before to be our ambassador: 100
    Say that the Emperor requests a parley
    Of warlike Lucius, and appoint the meeting
    Even at his father's house, the old Andronicus.

SATURNINUS

    Aemilius, do this message honourably,
    And if he stand in hostage for his safety,
    Bid him demand what pledge will please him best.

AEMILIUS

    Your bidding shall I do effectually.   *Exit*

TAMORA

    Now will I to that old Andronicus,
    And temper him with all the art I have
    To pluck proud Lucius from the warlike Goths.   110
    And now, sweet Emperor, be blithe again,
    And bury all thy fear in my devices.

SATURNINUS

    Then go incessantly, and plead to him.   *Exeunt*

＊

    Flourish. Enter Lucius with an army of Goths with   V.1
    drums and soldiers

LUCIUS

    Approvèd warriors and my faithful friends,
    I have receivèd letters from great Rome,

Which signifies what hate they bear their emperor,
And how desirous of our sight they are.
Therefore, great lords, be as your titles witness:
Imperious, and impatient of your wrongs,
And wherein Rome hath done you any scath
Let him make treble satisfaction.

FIRST GOTH

Brave slip, sprung from the great Andronicus,
10 Whose name was once our terror, now our comfort,
Whose high exploits and honourable deeds
Ingrateful Rome requites with foul contempt,
Be bold in us. We'll follow where thou lead'st,
Like stinging bees in hottest summer's day
Led by their master to the flowered fields,
And be avenged on cursèd Tamora.

ALL THE GOTHS

And as he saith, so say we all with him.

LUCIUS

I humbly thank him, and I thank you all.
But who comes here, led by a lusty Goth?

    Enter a Goth leading Aaron with his child in his arms

SECOND GOTH

20 Renownèd Lucius, from our troops I strayed
To gaze upon a ruinous monastery,
And as I earnestly did fix mine eye
Upon the wasted building, suddenly
I heard a child cry underneath a wall.
I made unto the noise, when soon I heard
The crying babe controlled with this discourse:
'Peace, tawny slave, half me and half thy dam!
Did not thy hue bewray whose brat thou art,
Had nature lent thee but thy mother's look,
30 Villain, thou mightst have been an emperor.
But where the bull and cow are both milk-white,

146

They never do beget a coal-black calf.
Peace, villain, peace!' – even thus he rates the
    babe –
'For I must bear thee to a trusty Goth,
Who, when he knows thou art the Empress' babe,
Will hold thee dearly for thy mother's sake.'
With this my weapon drawn, I rushed upon him,
Surprised him suddenly, and brought him hither
To use as you think needful of the man.

LUCIUS

O worthy Goth! This is the incarnate devil   40
That robbed Andronicus of his good hand;
This is the pearl that pleased your Empress' eye,
And here's the base fruit of her burning lust.
(*To Aaron*)
Say, wall-eyed slave, whither wouldst thou convey
This growing image of thy fiend-like face?
Why dost not speak? What, deaf? Not a word?
A halter, soldiers. Hang him on this tree,
And by his side his fruit of bastardy.

AARON

Touch not the boy, he is of royal blood.

LUCIUS

Too like the sire for ever being good.   50
First hang the child, that he may see it sprawl:
A sight to vex the father's soul withal.
Get me a ladder.
        A ladder is brought, which Aaron is made to climb
AARON   Lucius, save the child,
And bear it from me to the Empress.
If thou do this, I'll show thee wondrous things,
That highly may advantage thee to hear.
If thou wilt not, befall what may befall,
I'll speak no more but 'Vengeance rot you all!'

LUCIUS

Say on, and if it please me which thou speak'st,
60 Thy child shall live, and I will see it nourished.

AARON

And if it please thee? Why, assure thee, Lucius,
'Twill vex thy soul to hear what I shall speak:
For I must talk of murders, rapes, and
massacres,
Acts of black night, abominable deeds,
Complots of mischief, treason, villainies,
Ruthful to hear, yet piteously performed;
And this shall all be buried in my death,
Unless thou swear to me my child shall live.

LUCIUS

Tell on thy mind; I say thy child shall live.

AARON

70 Swear that he shall, and then I will begin.

LUCIUS

Who should I swear by? Thou believest no god.
That granted, how canst thou believe an oath?

AARON

What if I do not? As indeed I do not.
Yet for I know thou art religious
And hast a thing within thee callèd conscience,
With twenty popish tricks and ceremonies
Which I have seen thee careful to observe,
Therefore I urge thy oath. For that I know
An idiot holds his bauble for a god,
80 And keeps the oath which by that god he swears,
To that I'll urge him: therefore thou shalt vow,
By that same god, what god soe'er it be
That thou adorest and hast in reverence,
To save my boy, to nurse and bring him up,
Or else I will discover naught to thee.

LUCIUS

Even by my god I swear to thee I will.

AARON

First know thou, I begot him on the Empress.

LUCIUS

O most insatiate and luxurious woman!

AARON

Tut, Lucius, this was but a deed of charity
To that which thou shalt hear of me anon.   90
'Twas her two sons that murdered Bassianus;
They cut thy sister's tongue and ravished her,
And cut her hands and trimmed her as thou sawest.

LUCIUS

O detestable villain, call'st thou that trimming?

AARON

Why, she was washed and cut and trimmed, and
    'twas
Trim sport for them which had the doing of it.

LUCIUS

O barbarous, beastly villains, like thyself!

AARON

Indeed, I was their tutor to instruct them.
That codding spirit had they from their mother,
As sure a card as ever won the set.   100
That bloody mind I think they learned of me,
As true a dog as ever fought at head.
Well, let my deeds be witness of my worth:
I trained thy brethren to that guileful hole,
Where the dead corpse of Bassianus lay;
I wrote the letter that thy father found,
And hid the gold within that letter mentioned,
Confederate with the Queen and her two sons;
And what not done that thou hast cause to rue
Wherein I had no stroke of mischief in it?   110

V.1

<blockquote>

I played the cheater for thy father's hand,
And when I had it drew myself apart,
And almost broke my heart with extreme laughter.
I pried me through the crevice of a wall
When for his hand he had his two sons' heads,
Beheld his tears and laughed so heartily
That both mine eyes were rainy like to his;
And when I told the Empress of this sport,
She sounded almost at my pleasing tale,
And for my tidings gave me twenty kisses.

</blockquote>

A GOTH

<blockquote>

What, canst thou say all this and never blush?

</blockquote>

AARON

<blockquote>

Ay, like a black dog, as the saying is.

</blockquote>

LUCIUS

<blockquote>

Art thou not sorry for these heinous deeds?

</blockquote>

AARON

<blockquote>

Ay, that I had not done a thousand more.
Even now I curse the day – and yet I think
Few come within the compass of my curse –
Wherein I did not some notorious ill,
As kill a man or else devise his death,
Ravish a maid or plot the way to do it,
Accuse some innocent and forswear myself,
Set deadly enmity between two friends,
Make poor men's cattle break their necks,
Set fire on barns and haystacks in the night,
And bid the owners quench them with their tears.
Oft have I digged up dead men from their graves
And set them upright at their dear friends' door,
Even when their sorrows almost was forgot,
And on their skins, as on the bark of trees,
Have with my knife carvèd in Roman letters,
'Let not your sorrow die though I am dead'.

</blockquote>

150

But I have done a thousand dreadful things
As willingly as one would kill a fly,
And nothing grieves me heartily indeed
But that I cannot do ten thousand more.

LUCIUS

Bring down the devil, for he must not die
So sweet a death as hanging presently.

Aaron is brought down

AARON

If there be devils, would I were a devil
To live and burn in everlasting fire,
So I might have your company in hell
But to torment you with my bitter tongue.   150

LUCIUS

Sirs, stop his mouth and let him speak no more.

Aaron is gagged.

Enter Aemilius

A GOTH

My lord, there is a messenger from Rome
Desires to be admitted to your presence.

LUCIUS

Let him come near.
Welcome Aemilius. What's the news from Rome?

AEMILIUS

Lord Lucius, and you princes of the Goths,
The Roman Emperor greets you all by me,
And, for he understands you are in arms,
He craves a parley at your father's house,
Willing you to demand your hostages   160
And they shall be immediately delivered.

A GOTH

What says our general?

LUCIUS

Aemilius, let the Emperor give his pledges

Unto my father and my uncle Marcus,
And we will come. March away!   *Flourish. Exeunt*

V.2   *Enter Tamora disguised as Revenge, and her two sons,*
        Chiron as Rape and Demetrius as Murder

TAMORA
Thus, in this strange and sad habiliment,
I will encounter with Andronicus,
And say I am Revenge, sent from below
To join with him and right his heinous wrongs.
Knock at his study, where they say he keeps
To ruminate strange plots of dire revenge;
Tell him Revenge is come to join with him
And work confusion on his enemies.
        They knock and Titus opens his study door above

TITUS
Who doth molest my contemplation?
10 Is it your trick to make me ope the door,
That so my sad decrees may fly away,
And all my study be to no effect?
You are deceived, for what I mean to do
See here in bloody lines I have set down,
And what is written shall be executed.

TAMORA
Titus, I am come to talk with thee.

TITUS
No, not a word. How can I grace my talk,
Wanting a hand to give it action?
Thou hast the odds of me, therefore no more.

TAMORA
20 If thou didst know me, thou wouldst talk with me.

TITUS
I am not mad, I know thee well enough:

152

Witness this wretched stump, witness these crimson
    lines,
Witness these trenches made by grief and care,
Witness the tiring day and heavy night,
Witness all sorrow, that I know thee well
For our proud Empress, mighty Tamora.
Is not thy coming for my other hand?

TAMORA

Know, thou sad man, I am not Tamora.
She is thy enemy, and I thy friend.
I am Revenge, sent from th'infernal kingdom   30
To ease the gnawing vulture of thy mind
By working wreakful vengeance on thy foes.
Come down and welcome me to this world's light,
Confer with me of murder and of death.
There's not a hollow cave or lurking place,
No vast obscurity or misty vale
Where bloody murder or detested rape
Can couch for fear, but I will find them out,
And in their ears tell them my dreadful name,
Revenge, which makes the foul offender quake.   40

TITUS

Art thou Revenge? And art thou sent to me
To be a torment to mine enemies?

TAMORA

I am, therefore come down and welcome me.

TITUS

Do me some service ere I come to thee.
Lo by thy side where Rape and Murder stands.
Now give some surance that thou art Revenge:
Stab them, or tear them on thy chariot wheels,
And then I'll come and be thy waggoner,
And whirl along with thee about the globe,
Provide thee two proper palfreys, black as jet,   50

To hale thy vengeful waggon swift away,
And find out murderers in their guilty caves;
And when thy car is loaden with their heads,
I will dismount, and by thy waggon wheel
Trot like a servile footman all day long,
Even from Hyperion's rising in the east
Until his very downfall in the sea;
And day by day I'll do this heavy task,
So thou destroy Rapine and Murder there.

TAMORA

60   These are my ministers, and come with me.

TITUS

Are they thy ministers? What are they called?

TAMORA

Rape and Murder, therefore callèd so
'Cause they take vengeance of such kind of men.

TITUS

Good Lord, how like the Empress' sons they are,
And you the Empress. But we worldly men
Have miserable, mad, mistaking eyes.
O sweet Revenge, now do I come to thee,
And if one arm's embracement will content thee,
I will embrace thee in it by and by.   *Exit above*

TAMORA

70   This closing with him fits his lunacy.
Whate'er I forge to feed his brain-sick humours
Do you uphold and maintain in your speeches,
For now he firmly takes me for Revenge,
And being credulous in this mad thought,
I'll make him send for Lucius his son;
And whilst I at a banquet hold him sure,
I'll find some cunning practice out of hand
To scatter and disperse the giddy Goths,
Or at the least make them his enemies.

See, here he comes, and I must ply my theme.   80
    Enter Titus below

TITUS
Long have I been forlorn, and all for thee.
Welcome, dread Fury, to my woeful house;
Rapine and Murder, you are welcome too.
How like the Empress and her sons you are!
Well are you fitted, had you but a Moor.
Could not all hell afford you such a devil?
For well I wot the Empress never wags
But in her company there is a Moor,
And would you represent our Queen aright,
It were convenient you had such a devil.   90
But welcome as you are. What shall we do?

TAMORA
What wouldst thou have us do, Andronicus?

DEMETRIUS
Show me a murderer, I'll deal with him.

CHIRON
Show me a villain that hath done a rape,
And I am sent to be revenged on him.

TAMORA
Show me a thousand that hath done thee wrong,
And I will be revengèd on them all.

TITUS (*to Demetrius*)
Look round about the wicked streets of Rome,
And when thou find'st a man that's like thyself,
Good Murder, stab him: he's a murderer.   100
(*To Chiron*)
Go thou with him, and when it is thy hap
To find another that is like to thee,
Good Rapine, stab him: he is a ravisher.
(*To Tamora*)
Go thou with them, and in the Emperor's court

There is a queen attended by a Moor –
Well shalt thou know her by thine own proportion,
For up and down she doth resemble thee –
I pray thee, do on them some violent death:
They have been violent to me and mine.

TAMORA

110 Well hast thou lessoned us; this shall we do.
But would it please thee, good Andronicus,
To send for Lucius, thy thrice-valiant son,
Who leads towards Rome a band of warlike
    Goths,
And bid him come and banquet at thy house?
When he is here, even at thy solemn feast,
I will bring in the Empress and her sons,
The Emperor himself and all thy foes,
And at thy mercy shall they stoop and kneel,
And on them shalt thou ease thy angry heart.

120 What says Andronicus to this device?

TITUS

Marcus, my brother! 'Tis sad Titus calls.
    Enter Marcus
Go, gentle Marcus, to thy nephew Lucius.
Thou shalt enquire him out among the Goths.
Bid him repair to me and bring with him
Some of the chiefest princes of the Goths;
Bid him encamp his soldiers where they are.
Tell him the Emperor and the Empress too
Feast at my house, and he shall feast with them.
This do thou for my love, and so let him,

130 As he regards his agèd father's life.

MARCUS

This will I do, and soon return again.   *Exit*

TAMORA

Now will I hence about thy business,

And take my ministers along with me.

TITUS

Nay, nay, let Rape and Murder stay with me,
Or else I'll call my brother back again
And cleave to no revenge but Lucius.

TAMORA (*aside to her sons*)

What say you, boys? Will you abide with him
Whiles I go tell my lord the Emperor
How I have governed our determined jest?
Yield to his humour, smooth and speak him fair,   140
And tarry with him till I turn again.

TITUS (*aside*)

I knew them all, though they supposed me mad,
And will o'erreach them in their own devices,
A pair of cursèd hell-hounds and their dam.

DEMETRIUS

Madam, depart at pleasure, leave us here.

TAMORA

Farewell, Andronicus: Revenge now goes
To lay a complot to betray thy foes.

TITUS

I know thou dost, and sweet Revenge, farewell.

Exit Tamora

CHIRON

Tell us, old man, how shall we be employed?

TITUS

Tut, I have work enough for you to do.   150
Publius, come hither; Caius and Valentine.
     Enter Publius, Caius and Valentine

PUBLIUS

What is your will?

TITUS   Know you these two?

PUBLIUS

The Empress' sons, I take them: Chiron, Demetrius.

157

TITUS

 Fie, Publius, fie, thou art too much deceived:
 The one is Murder and Rape is the other's name.
 And therefore bind them, gentle Publius;
 Caius and Valentine, lay hands on them.
 Oft have you heard me wish for such an hour,
 And now I find it; therefore bind them sure,
160 And stop their mouths, if they begin to cry.   *Exit*

CHIRON

 Villains, forbear! We are the Empress' sons.

PUBLIUS

 And therefore do we what we are commanded.
   Publius, Caius and Valentine bind and gag Chiron
   and Demetrius
 Stop close their mouths, let them not speak a word.
 Is he sure bound? Look that you bind them fast.
   Enter Titus Andronicus with a knife, and Lavinia
   with a basin

TITUS

 Come, come, Lavinia; look, thy foes are bound.
 Sirs, stop their mouths. Let them not speak to me,
 But let them hear what fearful words I utter.
 O villains, Chiron and Demetrius,
 Here stands the spring whom you have stained with
  mud,
170 This goodly summer with your winter mixed.
 You killed her husband, and for that vile fault
 Two of her brothers were condemned to death,
 My hand cut off and made a merry jest,
 Both her sweet hands, her tongue, and that more dear
 Than hands or tongue, her spotless chastity,
 Inhuman traitors, you constrained and forced.
 What would you say if I should let you speak?
 Villains, for shame you could not beg for grace.

Hark, wretches, how I mean to martyr you:
This one hand yet is left to cut your throats,   180
Whiles that Lavinia 'tween her stumps doth hold
The basin that receives your guilty blood.
You know your mother means to feast with me,
And calls herself Revenge, and thinks me mad.
Hark, villains, I will grind your bones to dust,
And with your blood and it I'll make a paste,
And of the paste a coffin I will rear,
And make two pasties of your shameful heads,
And bid that strumpet, your unhallowed dam,
Like to the earth swallow her own increase.   190
This is the feast that I have bid her to,
And this the banquet she shall surfeit on:
For worse than Philomel you used my daughter,
And worse than Procne I will be revenged.
And now, prepare your throats. Lavinia, come,
Receive the blood, and when that they are dead,
Let me go grind their bones to powder small,
And with this hateful liquor temper it,
And in that paste let their vile heads be baked.
Come, come, be everyone officious   200
To make this banquet, which I wish may prove
More stern and bloody than the Centaurs' feast.
        He cuts their throats
So, now bring them in, for I'll play the cook,
And see them ready against their mother comes.
                              Exeunt with the bodies

        Enter Lucius, Marcus, and the Goths with Aaron V.3
        prisoner, and his child

LUCIUS

Uncle Marcus, since 'tis my father's mind

That I repair to Rome, I am content.

A GOTH

And ours with thine, befall what fortune will.

LUCIUS

Good uncle, take you in this barbarous Moor,
This ravenous tiger, this accursèd devil;
Let him receive no sust'nance, fetter him
Till he be brought unto the Empress' face
For testimony of her foul proceedings.
And see the ambush of our friends be strong:

10   I fear the Emperor means no good to us.

AARON

Some devil whisper curses in my ear,
And prompt me that my tongue may utter forth
The venomous malice of my swelling heart.

LUCIUS

Away, inhuman dog, unhallowed slave!
Sirs, help our uncle to convey him in.

    Flourish

The trumpets show the Emperor is at hand.

                Exeunt Goths with Aaron
    Sound trumpets. Enter Emperor and Empress with
    Aemilius, tribunes and others

SATURNINUS (*to Lucius*)

What, hath the firmament more suns than one?

LUCIUS

What boots it thee to call thyself a sun?

MARCUS

Rome's emperor and nephew, break the parle;

20   These quarrels must be quietly debated.
The feast is ready which the careful Titus
Hath ordained to an honourable end,
For peace, for love, for league and good to Rome;
Please you, therefore, draw nigh and take your places.

SATURNINUS

Marcus, we will.

Trumpets sounding. A table brought in. They sit. Enter
Titus like a cook, placing the dishes, and Lavinia with
a veil over her face, with young Lucius and others

TITUS

Welcome, my gracious lord; welcome dread Queen;
Welcome, ye warlike Goths; welcome, Lucius;
And welcome, all. Although the cheer be poor,
'Twill fill your stomachs. Please you eat of it.

SATURNINUS

Why art thou thus attired, Andronicus?   30

TITUS

Because I would be sure to have all well
To entertain your highness and your Empress.

TAMORA

We are beholden to you, good Andronicus.

TITUS

And if your highness knew my heart, you were.
My lord the Emperor, resolve me this:
Was it well done of rash Virginius
To slay his daughter with his own right hand
Because she was enforced, stained, and deflowered?

SATURNINUS

It was, Andronicus.

TITUS   Your reason, mighty lord?

SATURNINUS

Because the girl should not survive her shame,   40
And by her presence still renew his sorrows.

TITUS

A reason mighty, strong, and effectual;
A pattern, precedent, and lively warrant
For me, most wretched, to perform the like.

Unveils Lavinia

Die, die, Lavinia, and thy shame with thee,
And with thy shame thy father's sorrow die.
He kills her

SATURNINUS

What hast thou done, unnatural and unkind?

TITUS

Killed her for whom my tears have made me blind.
I am as woeful as Virginius was,

50 And have a thousand times more cause than he
To do this outrage, and it now is done.

SATURNINUS

What, was she ravished? Tell who did the deed.

TITUS

Will't please you eat? Will't please your highness
feed?

TAMORA

Why hast thou slain thine only daughter thus?

TITUS

Not I, 'twas Chiron and Demetrius:
They ravished her and cut away her tongue,
And they, 'twas they, that did her all this wrong.

SATURNINUS

Go, fetch them hither to us presently.

TITUS

Why, there they are, both bakèd in this pie,

60 Whereof their mother daintily hath fed,
Eating the flesh that she herself hath bred.
'Tis true, 'tis true, witness my knife's sharp point.
He stabs the Empress

SATURNINUS

Die, frantic wretch, for this accursèd deed.
He kills Titus

LUCIUS

Can the son's eye behold his father bleed?

There's meed for meed, death for a deadly deed.
> *He kills Saturninus. Uproar on stage. Enter Goths to*
> *protect the Andronici, who exit and go aloft*

MARCUS (*aloft*)
You sad-faced men, people and sons of Rome,
By uproars severed, as a flight of fowl
Scattered by winds and high tempestuous gusts,
O, let me teach you how to knit again
This scattered corn into one mutual sheaf,   70
These broken limbs again into one body,
Lest Rome herself be bane unto herself,
And she whom mighty kingdoms curtsy to,
Like a forlorn and desperate castaway,
Do shameful execution on herself.
But if my frosty signs and chaps of age,
Grave witnesses of true experience,
Cannot induce you to attend my words,
(*To Lucius*) Speak, Rome's dear friend, as erst our
        ancestor
When with his solemn tongue he did discourse   80
To lovesick Dido's sad-attending ear
The story of that baleful burning night
When subtle Greeks surprised King Priam's Troy.
Tell us what Sinon hath bewitched our ears,
Or who hath brought the fatal engine in
That gives our Troy, our Rome, the civil wound.
My heart is not compact of flint nor steel,
Nor can I utter all our bitter grief,
But floods of tears will drown my oratory
And break my utt'rance even in the time   90
When it should move ye to attend me most,
And force you to commiseration.
Here's Rome's young captain: let him tell the tale,
While I stand by and weep to hear him speak.

LUCIUS

>Then, gracious auditory, be it known to you
>That Chiron and the damnèd Demetrius
>Were they that murderèd our Emperor's brother,
>And they it were that ravishèd our sister.
>For their fell faults our brothers were beheaded,
100 >Our father's tears despised and basely cozened
>Of that true hand that fought Rome's quarrel out,
>And sent her enemies unto the grave.
>Lastly myself, unkindly banishèd,
>The gates shut on me and turned weeping out,
>To beg relief among Rome's enemies,
>Who drowned their enmity in my true tears
>And oped their arms to embrace me as a friend.
>I am the turned-forth, be it known to you,
>That have preserved her welfare in my blood,
110 >And from her bosom took the enemy's point,
>Sheathing the steel in my advent'rous body.
>Alas, you know I am no vaunter, I;
>My scars can witness, dumb although they are,
>That my report is just and full of truth.
>But soft, methinks I do digress too much,
>Citing my worthless praise. O, pardon me,
>For when no friends are by, men praise themselves.

MARCUS

>Now is my turn to speak. (*pointing to Aaron's child*)
>   Behold the child:
>Of this was Tamora deliverèd,
120 >The issue of an irreligious Moor,
>Chief architect and plotter of these woes.
>The villain is alive in Titus' house,
>And as he is to witness this is true,
>Now judge what cause had Titus to revenge
>These wrongs unspeakable, past patience,

Or more than any living man could bear.
Now have you heard the truth, what say you, Romans?
Have we done aught amiss, show us wherein,
And from the place where you behold us pleading
The poor remainder of Andronici   130
Will hand in hand all headlong hurl ourselves,
And on the raggèd stones beat forth our souls,
And make a mutual closure of our house.
Speak, Romans, speak, and if you say we shall,
Lo, hand in hand, Lucius and I will fall.

AEMILIUS

Come, come, thou reverend man of Rome,
And bring our emperor gently in thy hand,
Lucius, our emperor – for well I know
The common voice do cry it shall be so.

ROMANS

Lucius, all hail, Rome's royal emperor!   140

MARCUS (*to attendants*)

Go, go into old Titus' sorrowful house,
And hither hale that misbelieving Moor
To be adjudged some direful slaught'ring death
As punishment for his most wicked life.

      Exeunt Marcus, Lucius and attendants
    A long flourish. Enter Marcus and Lucius below

ROMANS

Lucius, all hail, Rome's gracious governor!

LUCIUS

Thanks, gentle Romans. May I govern so,
To heal Rome's harms, and wipe away her woe.
But, gentle people, give me aim awhile,
For nature puts me to a heavy task.
Stand all aloof, but uncle, draw you near   150
To shed obsequious tears upon this trunk.

   Kisses Titus

O, take this warm kiss on thy pale cold lips,
These sorrowful drops upon thy bloodstained face,
The last true duties of thy noble son.

MARCUS (*kissing Titus*)

Tear for tear and loving kiss for kiss,
Thy brother Marcus tenders on thy lips.
O, were the sum of these that I should pay
Countless and infinite, yet would I pay them.

LUCIUS (*to his son*)

Come hither, boy, come, come, and learn of us
160   To melt in showers. Thy grandsire loved thee well:
Many a time he danced thee on his knee,
Sung thee asleep, his loving breast thy pillow;
Many a story hath he told to thee,
And bid thee bear his pretty tales in mind,
And talk of them when he was dead and gone.

MARCUS

How many thousand times hath these poor lips,
When they were living, warmed themselves on thine!
O now, sweet boy, give them their latest kiss,
Bid him farewell, commit him to the grave,
170   Do them that kindness, and take leave of them.

YOUNG LUCIUS

O grandsire, grandsire, ev'n with all my heart
Would I were dead, so you did live again!
O Lord, I cannot speak to him for weeping;
My tears will choke me if I ope my mouth.

Enter attendants with Aaron

A ROMAN

You sad Andronici, have done with woes.
Give sentence on this execrable wretch
That hath been breeder of these dire events.

LUCIUS

Set him breast-deep in earth and famish him;

166

There let him stand and rave and cry for food.
If anyone relieves or pities him,   180
For the offence he dies. This is our doom.
Some stay to see him fastened in the earth.

AARON

Ah, why should wrath be mute and fury dumb?
I am no baby, I, that with base prayers
I should repent the evils I have done.
Ten thousand worse than ever yet I did
Would I perform if I might have my will.
If one good deed in all my life I did
I do repent it from my very soul.

LUCIUS

Some loving friends convey the Emperor hence,   190
And give him burial in his father's grave;
My father and Lavinia shall forthwith
Be closèd in our household's monument;
As for that ravenous tiger, Tamora,
No funeral rite, nor man in mourning weed,
No mournful bell shall ring her burial,
But throw her forth to beasts and birds to prey.
Her life was beastly and devoid of pity,
And being dead, let birds on her take pity.   *Exeunt*

Finis the Tragedy of Titus Andronicus

COMMENTARY

The abbreviations 'Q' and 'F' refer to readings common to all Quarto and Folio editions, unless otherwise specified. Quotations from other works by Shakespeare are followed by line reference to S. Wells and G. Taylor (eds.), *William Shakespeare: The Complete Works* (Oxford: Clarendon Press, 1986).

All relevant glosses have the support of the *Oxford English Dictionary*, M. P. Tilley's *A Dictionary of Proverbs in England in the Sixteenth and Seventeenth Centuries* (1950) and Gordon Williams's *A Glossary of Shakespeare's Sexual Language* (1997).

Title

The head-title in Q, *The Most Lamentable Romaine Tragedie of Titus Andronicus: As it was Plaide by the Right Honourable the Earle of Darbie, Earle of Pembrooke, and Earle of Sussex their Seruants*, is shortened in F to read, *The Lamentable Tragedy of Titus Andronicus*. There is no general consensus on whether the list of acting companies on the title-page in Q provides a chronological account of the early staging history of the play, or whether it simply implies that Sussex's Men hired actors who had previously worked for Derby (Lord Strange) or Pembroke for the short winter season of 1593–4.

I.1   The scene is located near the Temple of Jupiter or Capitol, which was the chief religious building of Rome. Even here, however, Shakespeare's Rome remains impressionistic, for he envisages the Capitol and the Senate House (or Curia) as adjacent buildings (see stage direction at line 66 below), or perhaps even as the same building. In fact they stood respectively on the Capitoline Hill, and in the Roman Forum below. The action is

divided into six major episodes: the dispute over the
succession (1–66); Titus's entry, the sacrifice of Alarbus
and the burial of his sons (67–159); the appointment of
Saturninus as Emperor with Lavinia as Empress (160–
278); the abduction of Lavinia, the killing of Mutius and
elevation of Tamora (279–340); the burial of Mutius
(341–401); and the formal reconciliation of the
Andronici with Saturninus (402–98).

0   (stage direction) *Flourish* a fanfare of trumpets, which
often marks an important entry or exit in F. The trum-
peters were usually placed in a curtained box called the
'music room' on part of the gallery above the stage.
tribunes constitutional officers elected to represent the ple-
beians in the state. The play, which blurs the distinctions
between Republican and Imperial Rome and has no specific historical location, disregards the fact that under the
emperors the function of the tribunes became nominal.
senators members of the ruling assembly of Rome, mostly
senior patricians, whose function became at best collab-
orative after the destruction of the Republic
aloft standard term in stage directions for the gallery,
also known as the balcony. The performances of the play
by the Earl of Sussex's Men recorded by Philip Henslowe
for 23 and 28 January and 6 February 1594 almost
certainly took place at the Rose Theatre. The recently
excavated foundations of the Rose show that Henslowe's
playhouse had a platform stage projecting into the audit-
orium from the wall of the tiring (or 'retiring') house.
The staging of the opening sequence of *Titus Andronicus*
requires two side doors, left and right in the wall, for the
entrance and exit of actors, perhaps a central opening
(see note to stage direction at line 92) and a gallery above
serving as an upper stage.
drums and colours drummers and standard-bearers

1–4   *Noble . . . swords.* Lines 1–2 are addressed to the senators
(patricians) in the gallery, lines 3–4 to those who have
entered with Saturninus below. Saturninus addresses the

senators because, as the representatives of the patricians,
they are more likely to support his claim to the succession
by right of primogeniture than the tribunes, who, as an
elected body, champion the principle of 'pure election'
(see note to line 16) and Bassianus's cause. Bassanius
invokes their protection at line 66.

1   *patrons* defenders. See also note to line 68.

4   *successive title* title to the succession

5   *his . . . that* of him who

8   *age* seniority

         indignity lack of respect resulting from having his claim
overlooked

10   *Caesar* title of Roman emperors

11   *Were gracious* found grace

12   *Keep . . . passage* guard . . . the route

         Capitol See head-note to I.1.

14   *consecrate* consecrated. The original punctuation in Q
and F is altered because this participle clearly governs
'virtue' on line 14, as well as the three abstract nouns on
line 15.

15   *continence* restraint (here both political and sexual). This
implicitly corrects Saturninus's facile use of 'justice' at
line 2.

16   *pure election* election only, unmixed with considerations
of primogeniture. 'Pure', however, retains its connotations of 'virtue' (line 14). Bassianus implies (a) that his
elder brother is given to a variety of vices, and (b) that
the principle of free election is at risk (line 17).

17   (stage direction) The Quarto instructs Marcus to enter
at the start of the scene with the tribunes and senators.
This edition follows the Folio, where Marcus's delayed
entrance is visually arresting and permits him to command the fray below.

19   *empery* imperial status

21   *special party* As a tribune of the people, Marcus represents an elective body, which was set by the Roman
constitution above the contention of political parties.

22   *In election* as a candidate in the election

23   *Pius* the 'surname', or honorary title given to Aeneas, the legendary founder of Rome

27   *accited* summoned

28   *Goths* a generic name for the allegedly 'barbarian' Germanic tribes existing outside the pale of Roman rule. Shakespeare's depiction of Rome is composite, so that evidence for dating the action of the play remains uncertain. From the perspective of the Gothic wars, however, the action could be located at any time between the end of the second century AD, when the weaknesses of an overextended frontier became apparent, and 410 AD, when the Visigothic king, Alaric, sacked Rome.

30   *yoked* tamed

35–8   *at this day ... Goths.* See An Account of the Text, pp. 230–31.

36   *monument* the tomb. See also lines 353–4 and notes to lines 92 and 95.

41   *flourishing in arms* The two terms of this phrase enrich each other: 'arms' adds to 'flourishing', in its usual sense of 'thriving' and 'prospering', the further sense of 'waving a weapon'; 'flourishing' imparts to 'arms' the double sense of 'weapons' and 'limbs'.

42–3   *by honour . . . succeed* out of respect for the reputation of him (the dead emperor) whom you wish to be succeeded decorously and meritoriously. The use of the word 'succeed' compacts two meanings: the princes should wish their father to 'be successful' in the only way a dead emperor can be, that is by being 'succeeded' worthily.

45   *pretend* claim

50   *so I do affy* I have such faith

58   (stage direction) Q and F provide an incomplete stage direction here – 'Exit soldiers' – and none at all at 62. It is, however, clear that whereas both Saturninus and Bassianus's soldiers leave to strengthen the massed entry at line 72, their followers remain on stage to make sense of the Captain's 'Roman, make way' at line 67.

64   *confident and kind* trusting and affectionate towards his
        kinsfolk

66   *competitor* candidate

68   *Patron* (a) defender; (b) pattern or model. This distinc-
        tion hardened only in the latter part of the seventeenth
        century.

71   *circumscribèd* fenced in

72   (stage direction) The omission of Alarbus from the
        Quarto and Folio stage directions is not enough to estab-
        lish that the incident of his sacrifice is a later addition.
        The error is sufficiently explained by the fact that he is a
        mute character. See An Account of the Text, pp. 230–31.

73   *mourning weeds* black apparel worn by widows

74   *his* its, as 'her' at line 76.

75   *lading* cargo. In Titus's metaphor, the dead sons brought
        back in exchange for the honour obtained.

77   *laurel* when woven into a crown, the emblem of victory

79   *tears* 'tears of grief', a meaning not obliterated by 'joy'
        of line 79. See also note to line 162.

80   *defender* Jove, also known as Jupiter Capitolinus. See
        head-note to I.1.

83   *Priam* The last king of Troy, whom Homer made the
        father of fifty sons.

86   *latest home* last home, the tomb. Proverbial.

87   The main clause of this line is 'let Rome reward', as
        suggested by the anaphora at lines 85–6.

89   *unkind* lacking in care and attention towards his kinsfolk.
        See note to line 64.

90–91   *Why . . . Styx* See Virgil, *Aeneid* VII.325–9: 'All this
        crowd thou seest is helpless and graveless . . . Nor may
        he [the grim ferryman, Charon] bear them o'er the
        dreadful banks and hoarse-voiced waters [of the river
        Styx] ere their bones have found a resting place. A
        hundred years they roam and flit about these shores.'

90   *suffer'st thou* do you allow, permit

92   *brethren* three syllables, also at lines 351 and 360
        (stage direction) The tomb of the Andronici is either

173

a building revealed through a central opening in the tiring-house wall, as indicated by lines 353–4, or a sepulchre suggested by raising the trap-door, as indicated by the phrase 'earthy prison' at line 102, or by the verb 'inter' at lines 149 and 378.

93   *greet* greet one another. The Roman family constituted a community of the living and the dead. See Introduction, p. 31.

95   *receptacle* This noun combines the ideas of 'place of shelter' (for the bodies of Titus's sons) and of 'receiving vessel' (for Titus's 'joys').

101   *Ad manes fratrum* to the shades of our brothers. This may be an echo from Livy's account of the heroic beginnings of Rome. In the first book of his *History*, he cites Horatius's words as he is about to dispatch the last of the three Curatii: '*duos . . . fratrum manibus dedi*' ('I have given two men to the shades of my brothers').

103   *the shadows* the dead. The 'unappeased' shadows of the dead frequently come back to haunt the living as ghosts in Shakespeare and his contemporaries.

104   *prodigies* ominous portents. The sacrifice of a high-ranking captive to free the souls of the dead from entrapment in the places of their physical existence was not, it seems, current Roman practice. Yet the example of Seneca's *Troades*, in which Pyrrhus sacrifices the captive Trojan princess Polyxena to placate the ghost of his father Achilles, and of the funeral rites of Pallas in Virgil's *Aeneid* IX, where prisoners are sacrificed and their blood sprinkled on the pyre (lines 81–2), persuaded the Renaissance that the custom was a Roman one. Shakespeare, for instance, refers to it in the Roman portion of one of his last plays, *Cymbeline*, at V.5.70–78. See Introduction, pp. 32–3.

107   (stage direction) That Tamora kneels is indicated by lines 457–8. That her sons should follow her example, however, is not required, despite the evidence of the Peacham drawing (from *c*.1595, now in the library at

Longleat), which is generally supposed to depict Tamora
and her sons kneeling to Titus and his sons, with a
defiant Aaron proudly erect.

109   *passion* violent grief

112   *Sufficeth not* is it not enough

113   *triumphs* triumphal processions

115   *in the streets* without ceremony. See also lines 457–8.

120–21   *Wilt thou . . . merciful* proverbial. That the Elizabethan
was meant to be responsive to this plea is shown by its
memorable amplification in Portia's address to Shylock
(*The Merchant of Venice*, IV.1.184–97) and Isabella's
plea to Angelo (*Measure for Measure*, II.2.60–65).

123   *Thrice-noble* 'Thrice' is a standard intensifier in Elizabethan English. See also 'thrice-valiant' at V.2.112.

125   *These . . . whom* these are the brothers of those whom

132   *clean* completely

133   *O cruel . . . piety* Tamora's remark is sharply ironic, as
she spurns both Titus's surname, 'Pius' (line 23), and
his perception of Alarbus's sacrifice as a religious and
pious deed.

134   *Scythia* a region east of the Danube described by the
Greek historian Herodotus as a land of bloodthirsty
tribesmen

135   *Oppose* compare. Demetrius implies that Rome outstrips
Scythia in barbarism.

139–41   *The selfsame gods . . . tent* in Ovid's *Metamorphoses*
XIII.533–75. Hecuba, wife of King Priam, survives the
sack and firing of Troy only to have her last remaining
son, Polydorus, murdered by the self-serving Polymes-
tor, the barbarian chief to whom she had entrusted him.
Failing to obtain justice from the victorious Greek leader,
Agamemnon, she receives the help of the gods in blinding
Polymestor, and in killing his sons with her own hands.
The extremity of her sufferings drives her into a 'mad-
ness' which ends by transforming her into a dog.

141   *Thracian* Thrace was an inland area west and north-west
of the Black Sea, populated with ferocious warlike tribes

regarded by antiquity as specially barbaric. Tereus, rapist of Philomela, was a Thracian. See Introduction, pp. 13, 35.

144   *quit* requite

    (stage direction) *with their swords bloody* This addition to the stage direction as it appears in Q and F is required by Lucius's call, 'See . . . how we have performed | Our Roman rites.'

146   *lopped* This participle echoes 'hew' in lines 100 and 132, and prepares a significant parallel with Lavinia's fate at II.4.17–18 ('lopped and hewed'), and subsequently.

148   *Whose smoke . . . sky*. See *Cymbeline*, V.5.476–8: 'Laud we the gods, | And let our crooked smokes climb to their nostrils | From our blest altars.'

150   *'larums* alarums. From the Italian *all' arma*, alarums were usually trumpet calls to arms.

154   *readiest* most eager. The elaborate alliteration, 'Rome's readiest' balanced by 'repose . . . rest', points up the antithesis.

155–8   *Secure . . . sleep*. A first draft of the famous dirge over the supposedly dead Imogen ('Fear no more the heat o' th' sun') in *Cymbeline* IV.2.258–80.

157   *drugs* plants from which poison may be extracted

162   *tributary* (a) offered in tribute, payment, bound as Lavinia is by ties of kinship to her brothers; (b) Lavinia's grief is flowing into and merging with her father's grief, like the waters of a tributary river into a larger one. Both Titus's and Lavinia's tears of grief (line 162) are mingled with tears of joy (line 164). See III.1.268 and note to line 79.

163   *obsequies* funeral ceremonies

169   *cordial* a potion invigorating the heart. Titus thanks Rome for having preserved ('reserved') Lavinia, as the distillation ('cordial') of Roman virtue, for his retirement. The name Cordelia in *King Lear* shares the same etymology.

171   *date* term of existence

173   *Gracious* finding favour

180   *Solon's happiness* According to Herodotus (*History* II, 82), Solon, hearing the fabulously wealthy Croesus boasting of his happiness, observed: 'Call no man happy till he be dead.' This remark became a classical commonplace and a Renaissance proverb.

185   *palliament* white robe. A neologism, probably compounded of two Latin words for 'robe': *pallium* and *paludamentum*. Its only other known occurrence is in George Peele's poem, 'The Honour of the Garter' (1593): 'A goodly king in robes most richly dight, | The upper like a Roman palliament'. This has been cited as evidence in favour of Peele's authorship of Act I of Shakespeare's play. See Introduction, p. 12.

186   *in election* See note to line 22.

188   *candidatus* chosen as candidate. A Latin word, from which 'candidate', that is 'clad in white', is derived. The Latin *candidus*, 'white', gives *candida*, 'toga', which signifies 'white robe' or 'palliament'.

192   *What* for what reason

195   *set abroad* set afoot

200   *In right and service* in service of the right

201–2 *Give . . . the world.* With this antithesis, Titus assumes, as Lear will, that symbols of honour can dispense with the reality of power.

204   *obtain and ask* obtain by asking. Proverbial: for Titus, to ask is to receive.

205   *canst thou tell?* can you anticipate the outcome (of the election)?

209   *shipped to hell* banished without possibility of recall

214   *wean . . . themselves* separate them from their immature preferences

219   *meed* reward

221   *ask your voices* ask that you put your votes at my disposal

224   *gratulate* salute

229–30 *Reflect . . . ripen justice* This remarkable expression of hope combines, in a single sentence, images of refulgence

('Reflect'), the sun-god ('Titan'), natural foison ('ripen') and integrity of rule ('justice'), that turn out to be comprehensively illusory.

233   *sort* social class. Marcus's formulation sounds facile, especially in view of Lavinia's remark at I.1.167.

236   (stage direction) F supplies a necessary stage direction here. The Romans must have left the upper-stage (the Senate) by the time Saturninus ascends again at line 301 as the newly elected emperor, accompanied by Tamora and her party, in order to emphasize the threatening presence of the Goths at the very heart of the main Roman political institution.

238   *us in our* Saturninus starts using the royal plural immediately after his election.

       election four syllables

239   *in part* as part

241   *onset* start

245   *Pantheon* Roman temple dedicated to all the gods

246   *motion* proposal

251   *consecrate* dedicate as to a sacred cause. Titus is not offering Saturninus literal gifts. There is no reason to assume, with some editors, that Titus has brought his chariot on stage.

253   *imperious* imperial

255   *ensigns* symbols

256   *father of my life* as Lavinia's father, hence future father-in-law, but also as Saturninus's deceased father, since his succession has been enabled by Titus's intercession. See also line 426.

259   *unspeakable* inexpressible

260   *fealty* loyalty

262   *for . . . state* for the sake of . . . status

264   *hue* appearance

267   *cheer* facial expression. The word alliterates with 'chance' and 'change'.

271–2   *he . . . | Can* he . . . who can

274   *sith* since

275   *Warrants* justifies

283   *Suum cuique* to each his own: proverbial and echoed in
       A Midsummer Night's Dream, III.2 458–9: 'And the
       country proverb known, | That every man should take
       his own'

285   (stage direction) The seven-line confrontation between
       Titus on the one hand, and Bassianus, Marcus and
       Lucius on the other, takes place in the vicinity of one of
       the stage doors, while the Goths, released by Saturninus
       at line 277 and the processional exit prompted by Satur-
       ninus at line 276 – 'Romans, let us go' – file through the
       other. In processional exits, the emperor would leave
       last, not first (see, for example, Mantegna's painting
       Triumph of Caesar at Hampton Court). Saturninus is
       therefore still on stage to reply to Titus's warning at line
       287: 'Treason, my lord! Lavinia is surprised.'

286   *avaunt* begone

287   *surprised* seized

289   (stage direction) Bassianus's assertion of prior right over
       Lavinia (lines 288–9) sounds very much like an exit
       line.

292   (stage direction) Saturninus is still close to his exit door:
       what Titus asks him to do is not to follow him, for the
       qualifying clause, 'and I'll soon bring her back', shows
       that Titus is going to deal with the kidnapping himself.
       Titus is rather asking Saturninus to follow the departed
       procession as if nothing had happened.

301   (stage direction) Saturninus's reappearance 'aloft' with
       Titus's former captives, as Titus remains below alone
       except for the body of the son he has killed 'for Rome',
       provides a powerful tableau of the catastrophic reversal
       of fortune that has occurred since Titus's triumphal
       entry.

304   *by leisure* hardly, only after careful and lengthy consider-
       ation, as opposed to 'never' in the next line

307   *stale* laughing-stock

312   *changing piece* fickle trollop. The term 'piece' is often

derogatory when applied to a woman, probably because it implies that she can be bought and sold. See, for example, *Twelfth Night*, I.5.24–6: 'If Sir Toby would leave drinking thou wert as witty a piece of Eve's flesh as any in Illyria.'

313   *flourished . . . sword* brandished (with overtones of 'swaggered') his sword in order to get her. See note to line 41.

315   *bandy* brawl, exchange blows

316   *ruffle* swagger

317   *words are razors* an intensification of the proverbial 'words cut like swords'

319   *Phoebe 'mongst her nymphs* Diana, goddess of chastity and the hunt, but here principally of the moon, among her maiden stars. Shakespeare may be remembering Phaer's 1558 translation of the *Aeneid* I.498–501:

> *Most like unto Diana bright when she to hunt goeth out*
>   *. . .*
> *Whom thousands of the lady nymphs await to do her will,*
> *She on her arms her quiver bears, and all them overshines.*

Only Saturninus's fatuous lubricity could associate Tamora with the goddess of chastity.

323   *Empress* three syllables

326   *sith* since

328   *Hymenaeus* Hymen, the Roman god of marriage

330   *climb* climb up to (as the Imperial Palace was traditionally on the Palatine Hill)

334   *handmaid* possibly an anticipation of the visual pun implied by the horrific stage action at the end of Act III, when Lavinia follows Titus off stage, carrying his hand between her teeth

339   *Whose wisdom* The antecedent is 'bride'.

340   *consummate . . . rites* complete the marriage ceremony

341   *bid to wait upon* invited to accompany, as a mark of respect

343   *challengèd* accused

350   *as becomes* as is fitting

351   *brethren* See note to line 92.

358   *impiety* echoes Tamora's charge at line 133

360   *brethren* See note to line 92.

363   *vouch it* maintain it (pronounced as if one syllable: 'vouch't')

367   *crest* (a) helmet, by association with the plume that embellished it; (b) heraldic device, placed above the shield and helmet of a coat of arms. Double metonymy for 'honour'.

369   *repute* reckon

375   *if . . . speed* if all the others are to prosper

379   *virtue's nest* an image of nurture. The tomb of the honoured dead is the birthplace of their virtue – an idea made explicit in line 393.

381   *be not barbarous* The deconstruction of the problematic opposition between Roman virtue and barbarous cruelty, which was initiated by Tamora at line 133, is developed further by Marcus at line 359 first and then here.

382   *upon advice* after deliberation

382–4   *Ajax . . . funerals* In a fit of madness this Homeric Greek warrior attacked and killed a flock of sheep imagining them to be the Greek generals who had slighted him. When he recovered his senses he committed suicide. Ulysses, the son of Laertes, persuaded the Greek *supremo*, Agamemnon, to grant Ajax honourable burial.

391   *trophies* honorific memorials

392   (speech prefix) The exclusion of Titus from this little ceremony by later editors, in contradiction of the explicit direction of the early editions, is not warranted. Lines 386–9 show Titus to have capitulated, albeit gracelessly. Indeed, by the beginning of the third act, he includes Mutius among the sons who have 'died in honour's lofty bed' (III.1.10–11).

394   *dumps* bouts of melancholy

395   *subtle* crafty, calculating

399   *the man* Titus himself

401   MARCUS . . . *remunerate*. This line is absent from Q and has no speech prefix in F. Although the line seems in keeping with Marcus's attempt to reassure Titus, its origins remain doubtful.

      (stage direction) The entrance of Titus's sons with the newly wed Bassianus and Lavinia balances the entrance, at the opposite door, of the newly wed Saturninus and Tamora, with her two sons and Aaron. In Q, the symmetry of this entrance is mirrored by the layout of the stage direction, thus:

Enter the Emperour, Tamora   *Enter at the other doore*
and her two sonnes, with the   *Bascianus and Lavinia*
Moore at one doore.   *with others.*

402   *played your prize* won your game. Usually used of fencing, Saturninus implies that Lavinia is some brawler's moll.

407   *rape* abduction

411   *that* that which

412–13   *You are . . . you* a pointed adaptation of a common proverb: 'all that is sharp is short'

419   *opinion* reputation

423   *controlled . . . gave* curbed in what he gave so freely; 'controlled' suggests 'rebuking' as well as 'reining in'

427   *leave . . . deeds* stop justifying my actions

436   *put it up* sheathe the weapon, put up with the insult. A distant echo of line 402: Bassianus has fought his bout successfully; Saturninus is not even allowed to begin his.

437   *forfend* forbid

438   *author to dishonour you* responsible for dishonouring you

439   *undertake* vouch

441   *not dissembled* that Titus is unable to control, and therefore conceal. Titus's 'fury' in killing his son is a true expression of his 'griefs' on behalf of his own and the Emperor's honour.

443   *vain suppose* empty supposition

446   *Dissemble . . . discontents.* In open contrast with line 441.

452   *at entreats* to entreaties
       let me alone leave the rest to me

460   *Take up* raise to his feet. Titus has been kneeling for 30
       lines.

465   *incorporate in Rome* incorporated into the body of Rome

477   (stage direction) Bassianus may or may not kneel here.
       Tamora's lines at 471–3 seems to imply that she has
       already obtained Saturninus's pardon on his behalf.
       However, Tamora's failure to mention Bassianus as one
       of the kneeling petitioners at line 483 is no indication
       that Bassianus should therefore be standing, as Lavinia,
       who is explicitly invited to kneel at lines 474–5, is not
       mentioned either.

479   *Tend'ring* having regard for

489   *like a churl* 'as if I were a rustic', if referred to Saturninus
       himself, or 'selfishly, like a miser', if referred to Lavinia

490   *sure as death* proverbial

494   *love-day* (a) a day appointed by the Church for settling
       disputes and restoring amity (Saturninus has been cued
       by Tamora's declaration at line 468); (b) a day devoted
       to love

498   *gramercy* great thanks. Saturninus matches Titus's '*bon-
       jour*' at line 497 with more French *politesse*.

498   (stage direction) Q has no act-division so Aaron remains
       on stage and comes forward to break his silence. In F,
       which marks act breaks, Aaron leaves with the others
       to return immediately in order to open Act II. This
       procedure violates Elizabethan stage conventions, which
       discourage immediate returns. This edition retains F's
       act-division, as opposed to assimilating Act II, scene 1
       into Act I, as has been recently proposed, in order to
       stress the transition to a new episode, but departs from
       F by keeping Aaron on stage.

II.1   The figure of Aaron is used to establish an unbroken
            continuity between Act I and II, but the form of his first
            speech (a soliloquy to the audience), its style (exotic
            hyperbole) and its content (Machiavellian naturalism)
            represent so unexpected a development that it effectively
            announces a new act by taking us into a new world. By
            the end of the speech, though we are still in Rome we
            have been distanced from the Capitol, and we are ready
            to accept that Demetrius and Chiron have been able to
            become rivals in their pursuit of Lavinia. The scene
            is divided into three parts: Aaron's soliloquy (1–25);
            Demetrius's and Chiron's rivalry for Lavinia (26–98);
            and Aaron's solution to their problems (99–135).

1   *Olympus* snow-capped mountain on the borders of Thes-
            saly in northern Greece, regarded as the abode of the
            gods

3   *of* from

7   *Gallops the zodiac* gallops through the zodiac, a belt in
            the celestial sphere extending on each side of the circle
            traced in the heavens by the apparent orbit of the sun
            coach Phaeton or Helios, the sun-god, was thought to
            drive a golden chariot daily across the sky.

8   *overlooks* looks down on

14   *mount her pitch* ascend to the apex of her flight. 'Pitch' is
            a term in falconry denoting the position from which the
            falcon swoops down on his prey; but, given the insistent
            repetition of 'mount', erotic overtones become audible.

14–15   *triumph . . . prisoner* Aaron's rivalry with Titus surfaces
            explicitly here.

17   *Prometheus . . . Caucasus* Prometheus was the son of a
            Titan, who stole fire from the heaven for the use of
            mankind. Zeus punished him for his presumption by
            chaining him to a cliff face in the Caucasus, and by
            having an eagle or vulture devour his liver every day.
            The sado-masochism of the image here is not accidental.

18   *weeds* garments

22   *Semiramis* legendary Assyrian queen, who became a by-word for opulent voluptuousness and cruelty
        nymph lesser goddess, inhabitant of trees and rivers, but, more generally, sexually desirable woman

23   *siren* mythological temptress whose magic songs lured sailors to their death; hence 'charm' in this line and 'shipwreck' in the next

25   *storm* Aaron redirects the associations of 'shipwreck' by punningly alluding to the noisy entry of the brothers.
        (stage direction) *braving* defying each other. The quarrel between Demetrius and Chiron is a parody of the rivalry between Saturninus and Bassianus (see lines 31–2 and 73–4 below).

26   *edge* sharpness

27   *graced* shown favour

28   *affected* loved

29   *dost overween* are presumptuous

30   *to bear me down with braves* to overwhelm me with blustering threats

32   *gracious* worthy of favour, thus echoing the claim made at line 27

35   *approve* prove

36   *plead* demonstrate (a legal term)

37   *Clubs* truncheons. Aaron is parodying the call for officers to check a public brawl. Compare the Lord Mayor's 'I'll call for clubs, if you will not away', *1 Henry VI*, I.3.84.

39   *dancing-rapier* ornamental sword worn at social assemblies

40   *so . . . to* so . . . as to

41   *Go to* a phrase expressing derisive incredulity
        lath toy sword. Pun on Chiron's sexual inexperience.

46   *So near . . . draw* In Elizabethan times, acts of violence performed 'within the verge', that is a circle with a radius of twelve miles surrounding the person of the sovereign wherever she went, were regarded as especially transgressive and fell under the jurisdiction of her coroner, and not under that of the local authorities.

48 *wot* know

53 *put up* put away your weapons

60 *Away* stop it. A standard exclamation.

62 *brabble* brawl

64 *jet upon* encroach on

67 *broached* started

68 *controlment* imposition of authority

70 *discord's ground* (a) the cause of this quarrel; (b) the bass melody of this inharmonious music

71–2 *all the world:* | *... all the world* This repetition emphasizes Chiron's naïve eagerness, which Demetrius remarks upon at line 41.

73 *meaner* of lower rank

75 *in Rome* The play observes a notional distinction between Roman strictness and Gothic licence.

80 *propose* offer to face

81 *Why ... strange?* why do you think it so difficult? As in *Two Gentlemen of Verona*, I.2.99.

82–7 Demetrius off-loads a stock of proverbs. The proverbial expression at lines 82–3 is frequent in early Shakespeare, see, for example, *Richard III*, I.2.215–16: 'Was ever woman in this humour wooed? | Was ever woman in this humour won?'; *1 Henry VI*, V.3.78–9: 'She's beautiful, and therefore to be wooed; | She is a woman, therefore to be won'; and Sonnet 41: 'Gentle thou art, and therefore to be won; | Beauteous thou art, therefore to be assailed'.

89 *Vulcan's badge* the cuckold's horns. Vulcan, the lame god of fire and the master blacksmith, was married to Venus, the goddess of love, and became cuckolded by Mars, the god of war.

91 *to court it* how to play the suitor

94 *cleanly* neatly, as in 'he got clean away'. Demetrius is inadvertently sounding the first note of the motif of the 'hunting' of Lavinia, which Aaron will elaborate at lines 112–18.

95 *snatch* quick theft, but also quick copulation

96   *turns* purposes, but also 'copulation', from the common expression 'to serve a turn', meaning 'to copulate'

97   *hit it . . . hit it* Demetrius means 'understood the point'; Aaron, punning brutally, means 'hit the target', that is 'enjoyed Lavinia'.

100   *square* quarrel

101   *speed* succeed

103   *join for that you jar* unite to achieve what makes you clash

104   *policy* machination

105   *That you affect* what you desire

106–7   *what you . . . may* proverbial

108   *Lucrece* The wife of a Roman patrician, she was raped by the son of Tarquin, seventh king of Rome, and stabbed herself to death. As a result, Rome banished the Tarquins, abolished the monarchy and became a republic. Shakespeare wrote *The Rape of Lucrece* (1594) soon after *Titus Andronicus*.

110   *than ling'ring languishment* decisive repudiation of courtly love's cultivation of service as romantic fulfilment

111   *path* solution, developing from 'speedier course' at line 110

112   *solemn* formal, as befits a royal entertainment

115   *plots* places, pieces of land

116   *kind* nature

117   *Single* hunting term, for the picking out of a particular quarry

120   *sacred* deliberately blasphemous, as is the participle 'consecrate' in the next line

123   *file our engines* sharpen our plots. This phrase brings to a climax the passage of Machiavellian diction introduced by 'policy' at line 104.

124   *square yourselves* quarrel with each other, and so foil your purposes

125   *wishes' height* This phrase echoes Aaron's plan to 'arm [his] heart' and 'mount' Tamora's 'pitch' in his soliloquy at the beginning of Act II.

126   *house of fame* The title of a well-known poem by Chaucer,

but Shakespeare probably alludes to Ovid's *Metamorphoses* XII.39–63, which evokes a house in which silence, privacy and secrecy do not exist, for it is honeycombed with a thousand apertures, and filled with a ceaseless murmur of gossip and report.

129   *strike . . . turns* See note to line 96.

131   *treasury* maidenhead

133   *Sit fas aut nefas* (Latin) be it right or wrong

134   *fits* seizures, convulsions

135   *Per Stygia, per manes vehor* (Latin) I am borne across the Styx, and through the shades of the dead, that is 'I remain in hell'. Both Latin phrases evoke the language of Phaedra's last speech in Seneca's *Hippolytus*. Thomas Kyd's *The Spanish Tragedie* popularized a fashion for quoting Latin tags in tragedies.

II.2   In contrast to the previous scene, this short scene set outside the imperial palace offers preparations for the day's bona fide hunting.

0   (stage direction) *noise with hounds and horns* Hounds were sometimes introduced on to the Elizabethan stage, as were hunting horns, but 'noise' suggests a group of instruments playing off stage.

1   *morn* The alternative reading 'moon' preserved in Q1–2 is normally discarded. It is, however, worth noting that 'moon' establishes a further link between the imagery of the love-chase introduced by Aaron in the previous scene and the royal hunt which is about to start here, as the moon was traditionally associated with Diana, the maiden goddess of hunting. See also II.3.57–65.

3   *uncouple* set the hounds free
bay prolonged barking

5   *hunter's peal* horn-blowing to set the dogs barking. See also line 13.

9   *troubled in my sleep* Titus had premonitory dreams and is concerned about the Emperor's safety.

21 *chase* hunting ground

24 *run like swallows* The subject is 'horse' (collective). The phrase is proverbial. Compare Aaron at IV.2.171: 'Now to the Goths, as swift as swallow flies'.

26 *dainty doe* Lavinia. See II.1.117.

II.3 This scene is located in the royal forest or hunting park. It is divided into six episodes: Aaron's divulsion to Tamora of his plot against the Andronici (1–54); Tamora's taunting by Bassianus and Lavinia (55–88); the killing of Bassianus (89–117); Lavinia's vain pleas (118–91); the entrapment of Martius and Quintus (192–245); and their inculpation for Bassianus's death by Aaron and Tamora (246–306). The pit is the dominant image of this scene. It is not only a hunting trap, as at lines 193 or 224. It is associated with (a) hell: see note to line 98, and Martius's allusion to 'Cocytus' misty mouth' (236), one of the foggy rivers of the underworld; (b) the grave: see, for example, references to the 'loathsome pit' (176) invoked by Lavinia as a shelter from Chiron and Demetrius's 'worse-than-killing lust', the 'detested, dark, blood-drinking pit' (224), in which Bassianus lies, or the 'fell devouring receptacle' (235), which echoes Titus's description of the tomb of the Andronici as the 'sacred receptacle of [his] joys' at I.1.95; and, more complexly, with (c) 'entrails' (230), the 'swallowing womb' (239) and female genitalia (198–201).

2 *under a tree* As Henslowe's *Diary* shows, property trees and 'moss banks' were used on the barren Elizabethan stage. The burying of gold to frame an innocent person occurs in Ovid's *Metamorphoses* XIII.58–60, where Ajax alleges that Ulysses, in revenge for having been unmasked as a malingerer by Palamedes, produces gold he has hidden himself to prove that his denouncer has taken bribes.

3 *inherit* possess

5   *coin* (a) fabricate; (b) by means of coins (referring to Aaron's use of a bag of gold coins to frame Titus)

8   *repose . . . unrest* A widespread Elizabethan paradox put into circulation by Kyd's *The Spanish Tragedie*, I.3.5: 'Then rest we heere a while in our unrest.' See also *Titus*, IV.2.31.

9   *That . . . chest* the beneficiaries of Tamora's treasury, that is the Andronici, who are now dependent on Tamora

12–14 *The birds . . . wind* See Seneca's *Hippolytus*, 5088–9: 'Wherein the complaining birds make music, and the ash-trees and ancient beeches quiver, moving gently in the breeze'.

13   *snakes lies* common Elizabethan concordance of a third person singular verb with a plural noun

19   *double hunt* Compare *Venus and Adonis*, 695–6: 'Echo replies, | As if another chase were in the skies.' In the play, this image is ironic, pointing to the two simultaneous hunts.

20   *yellowing* yelping, an extension of 'yell'

22–4   *wand'ring prince . . . cave* See Virgil's *Aeneid* IV, where Aeneas, in the course of his wanderings between his escape from Troy and his foundation of Rome, sojourns in Carthage where its queen, Dido, falls in love with him. In Book IV.160–72, the royal couple, surprised by a storm during a day's hunting, find shelter and solace in a convenient cave.

28–9   *nurse's song . . . asleep* Compare *Venus and Adonis*, 973–4: 'By this, far off she hears some huntsman's hollo; | A nurse's song ne'er pleased her babe so well'. Following the previous parallel with *Venus and Adonis* (see line 19 above), and Aaron's explicit identification of his mistress with the goddess of love at line 30, the play links Tamora with Venus, as it has associated Lavinia with Lucrece.

31   *Saturn* Roman version of the Greek god Kronos, father of time and devourer of his children in an attempt to foil a prediction that he would be deposed by one of them.

In his planetary form he renders those born under his sign vengeful and unforgiving.

34–6   *My fleece ... execution?* Aaron is associated with the serpent who tempted Eve, as he provokes Tamora to collaborate in his crimes.

37   *venereal* having the character of Venus

39   *Blood ... head.* This metaphor occurs four times in Thomas Lodge's *The Wounds of Civil War*, at II.1.84; II.1.187; III.4.63; V.1.42. See Introduction, pp. 38, 42.

41   *never ... in thee* Aaron takes literally the courtly lover's hyperbole that his mistress promises paradise, a trope which Berowne calls 'pure, pure idolatry' in *Love's Labour's Lost*, IV.3.73.

43   *Philomel* Ovid's account of the rape of Philomela (*Metamorphoses* VI.424–674) is a central source, model and theme of the play. See note to IV.1.47–8 and Introduction, pp. 13–14.

47   *fatal-plotted scroll* letter containing a death-dealing plot, implicating Titus's sons, Quintus and Mutius, as the killers of Bassianus. See line 294.

49   *parcel of our hopeful booty* part of our anticipated loot

56   *Unfurnished ... troop?* indecorously deprived of her attendants

57   *Dian, habited like her* As goddess of the chase, the virginal Diana wore a hunting garment of great simplicity. Bassianus, however, has seen Aaron with her (line 48), and he sarcastically implies that her resemblance to the goddess is confined to her habit.

60   *Saucy controller* impudent inspector

61–4   *Had I ... limbs* Ovid's *Metamorphoses* III.138–253 describes how a young prince, Actaeon, hunting in the woods surprised Diana and her maidens bathing, how the outraged goddess turned him into an antlered stag, and how he was run down and killed by his own hounds. Tamora's ferocious appropriation of Bassianus's gibe covertly assumes the very power she disclaims, and thus promises an enactment of the same inverted hunt.

64   *drive* rush

66   *Under your patience* ironically polite

67–71   *horning . . . stag* Cuckolded husbands were fancifully said
        to wear horns on the brow (by analogy with rutting stags
        frequently deprived of their does by stronger inter-
        lopers). This allows Lavinia to query Tamora's appropri-
        ation of the Actaeon myth, by converting Bassianus as
        quarry into Saturninus as cuckold.

68   *doubted* suspected

72   *Cimmerian* Homer placed the mythical Cimmerians
        beyond the sunset, in total darkness.

74   *Spotted* soiled

83   *joy* enjoy

86   *noted* notorious

91–108 *Have . . . miserable death* Tamora's description of the
        valley seems to be entirely unrelated to her previous
        account of it (10–29). The change is not merely the
        effect of a change in mood (incitement to crime instead
        of invitation to love): the description is as conventional
        in its iconography (it assembles the tropes of the land-
        scape of hell) as was its predecessor (variations on the
        tropes of the *locus amoenus*).

92   *'ticed* enticed

95   *O'ercome* overgrown
        baleful mistletoe So-called by association with the legend
        that the Scandinavian god of peace, Balder, was slain by
        an arrow made of mistletoe.

97   *fatal raven* The croak of the raven was thought to presage
        death.

98   *this abhorrèd pit* The first of several references to the pit.
        Here the pit is associated with hell, as line 105 confirms.
        It would be represented on stage by the open trapdoor,
        perhaps partly covered with foliage. See II.3.199–200.

101   *urchins* hedgehogs

104   *straight* immediately

107   *dismal yew* (a) sombre, cheerless; (b) unpropitious

118   *Semiramis* See note to II.1.22.

120   *poniard* dagger

122   *here is more belongs to her* she owns something in addition to her life (her chastity)

123   *First thrash the corn . . . straw* proverbial; 'thresh corn' was a common term for sexual intercourse.

126   *quaint* fastidious. The original reading in Q and F, 'painted', is obviously inappropriate as Demetrius and Chiron must believe Lavinia to be chaste, since they plan to spoil her chastity.

131   *honey* sexual sweets. This image prompts 'wasp' and 'sting' at line 132.

      ye desire Recent editors sometimes retain the original reading provided by Q and F1, that is 'we desire', since Lavinia's defilement is something both Tamora and her sons desire. This edition follows F2 in order to emphasize Tamora's wish to dispatch Lavinia immediately, which is first expressed at lines 120–21 and reiterated at line 132.

132   *Let . . . outlive . . . sting.* This is the only known instance in Elizabethan English in which the verb 'outlive' (survive) is used intransitively, as a result of a necessary emendation of the original punctuation. See Collation 4.

133   *warrant* one syllable

135   *nice-preservèd honesty* chastity fastidiously preserved

140–41 *be your heart . . . rain* combination of two proverbial expressions: 'a heart as hard as flint' and 'constant dropping wears a stone'

146   *not sons alike* children unlike their mother, as Chiron's reply suggests. See next note.

148   *prove . . . bastard* (a) show myself an undutiful son (by failing to heed my mother's teaching); (b) show myself genetically illegitimate (by possessing virtues incompatible with hers)

149   *raven . . . lark* proverbial. See also note to III.1.158.

151–2 *The lion . . . all away.* In Aesop, a lion who paid court to a farmer's daughter had his claws pared and his teeth pulled because the girl was frightened of him. By Shakespeare's time, the fable had turned into a proverb.

153–4   *ravens . . . nests* Compare *The Winter's Tale*, II.3.186–7: 'Some powerful spirit instruct the kites and ravens | To be thy nurses!'

154   *birds* chicks

171–9   This exchange is coded in terms of begging and paying. Lavinia, describing herself as 'Poor I' (171), is a pitiful beggar (170) in that she is reduced to begging for death (170, 173). This 'compassion' threatens to turn Tamora into a 'charitable murderer' (178). Thus Lavinia, herself reduced to a paradox (begging for *nothingness*), seeks to convert Tamora into an oxymoron. Tamora repudiates this appeal at line 179 by trumping Lavinia's 'charity' with her sons' *fee*.

172   *fond* foolish

174   *denies* forbids

179   *fee* reward. Lavinia's defilement is Chiron and Demetrius's recompense for carrying out Tamora's orders (114–15) by killing Bassianus.

181   *stayed* delayed

183   *our general name* the good name of women

187   *sure* secure, unable to cause harm

189   *made away* killed off

191   *spleenful* lustful. The spleen was regarded as the seat of passion.

      trull harlot

192   *better foot before* proverbial, 'put your best foot forward'. Quintus and Martius enter as if drugged. They fall into the pit partly because of Aaron's misdirection, but chiefly because of their weakness. Their condition may have been partly suggested by Thyestes's sensation of impotence in Seneca's play of that name. Shakespeare had *Thyestes* in mind as he wrote *Titus* (see note to V.2.193–4). As Thyestes approaches the longed-for Argos and the appalling fate it has prepared for him, his body and spirit falter: 'I want to go on, but my limbs are unsteady

with sluggish knees, and I am borne back helplessly from
where I seek to go' (lines 436–7). See Introduction, p. 39.

208   *made away* See note to line 189.

210   *unhallowed* unsanctified

211   *surprisèd . . . fear* bewildered by an uncanny terror

219   *by surmise* by mere imagining

222   *berayed* defiled

223   *on a heap* prostrate

227   *ring . . . hole* a reference to the belief that rubies and
garnets emitted their own light

228   This simile suggests that the pit is in ambiguous relationship with the tomb of the Andronici. This is reinforced
by the application of the term 'receptacle' to both: the
pit at line 235, and the tomb at I.1.89.

229   *earthy* earth-coloured

230   *ragged entrails* rough interior

231   *Pyramus* The story of Pyramus and Thisbe is derived
from Ovid's *Metamorphoses* (IV.55–156). Neighbouring
adolescents fall in love, but being forbidden to see each
other, make an assignation outside the city. The girl,
Thisbe, arrives first, but seeing a lioness with bloody
jaws, runs away, leaving her cloak which the animal tears
to pieces. The boy, Pyramus, discovers the garment
and drawing the too-obvious conclusion, kills himself. Thisbe returns, finds her dying lover and also
kills herself. The tale was regarded as a model of pathos,
not least by Nick Bottom in *A Midsummer Night's
Dream*.

238–9   *Or, wanting . . . plucked* or that, if I lack the strength to
hoist you out of the pit, I may be pulled down myself

239   *womb* 'stomach' as well as 'matrix'. Everything in the
immediate context, including the epithet 'swallowing',
suggests that the idea of 'stomach' remains present. The
pit, which has been presented as the lair of the panther,
consistently attracts images of ingestion: mouth (199),
blood (200), blood-stainèd (210), blood-drinking (224),
entrails (230), devouring (235), mouth (236), swallowing

(239), gaping (249). Moreover, the stage action requires the trapdoor to 'swallow' three men in rapid succession: Bassianus, Martius and Quintus. What presides over this scene is Nature the Devourer.

246   *Along* come along
255   *chase* See note to II.2.21.
258   *out* an all-purpose intensifier
262   *search* probe
264   *writ* the letter introduced at line 46
265   *complot . . . timeless* plot of this untimely
266   *fold* hide in smiles
268   *handsomely* readily at hand, conveniently
272   *elder tree* associated with Judas who hanged himself from an elder
275   *purchase* win
281   *kind* nature, but with a strong implication of 'family'. See note to I.1.64 and I.1.89
294   *Andronicus . . . up.* Tamora must have refined on Aaron's plan (see II.3.46–7) by dropping the letter opportunely for Titus to pick it up.
295   *bail* Titus offers himself as 'bail'. This pre-shadows the sacrifice of his hand as 'ransom' at III.1.150 ff.
298   *their suspicion* the allegations contained in the letter
305   *Fear not* do not be afraid for

II.4   In performance this scene would be continuous with its predecessor. In its response to Lavinia's mutilations, it exhibits two starkly contrasting kinds of verbal inventiveness at 1–10 and 11–57; a third kind is reserved for Titus in the next scene. For a detailed discussion of the subtext of Marcus's speech at 11–57, see Introduction, pp. 17–22.

3   *bewray* reveal
5   *scrawl* gesticulate, with a possible anticipation of the modern meaning, 'to write or draw carelessly'
6   *sweet* scented

8   *silent walks* paths for meditation, but also a vicious allusion to Lavinia's mutilated tongue

9   *cause* case

10   *knit* knot

12   *Cousin* generic term used for any family relation beyond immediate kinship

13   *would all . . . wake me* I would give all my wealth to be awake. See also III.1.251.

14   *strike* astrological term signifying 'blast by malign (stellar) influence'

22–5   *a crimson river . . . honey breath* Compare *The Rape of Lucrece*, lines 1734–41:

> *And from the purple fountain Brutus drew*
> *The murderous knife, and as it left the place,*
> *Her blood, in poor revenge, held it in chase;*
> *And bubbling from her breast, it doth divide*
> *In two slow rivers, that the crimson blood*
> *Circles her body in on every side,*
> *Who like a late-sack'd island vastly stood*
> *Bare and unpeopled in this fearful flood.*

Lavinia's mutilation is rendered in terms of pastoral spoilation: branches (18), shadows (19), river (22), fountain (23), Titan (31), cloud (32), lily (44) and aspen leaves (45). The imagery of this passage is in keeping with the larger dualism of park and wilderness introduced in II.2.12–20 and 93–104.

26   *Tereus* King of Thrace, who raped his sister-in-law, Philomela, in the woods, cutting out her tongue to secure his safety. See note to II.3.43.

27   *detect* expose

30   *a conduit . . . spouts* graphic description of Lavinia's mutilated, bleeding arms and mouth, in contrast with the register and the pastoral imagery used in Marcus's speech

31–2   *red as Titan . . . cloud* Compare *Richard II*, III.3.63–6:

> *As doth the blushing discontented sun*
> *From out the fiery portal of the east,*
> *When he perceives the envious clouds are bent*
> *To dim his glory . . .*

34   *heart* the seat of thoughts as well as feelings

36–7   *Sorrow . . . where it is* proverbial

38   *Philomela* See Introduction, pp. 13–14.

39   *in a tedious . . . mind* in a laboriously sewn embroidery conveyed what was in her mind. See note to II.3.43.

43   *Philomel* See note to II.3.43.

44   *lily* lily-white

45   *aspen leaves* proverbial. Poplar leaves are responsive to the softest wind.

47   *for his life* for fear of being struck dead

51   *Thracian poet* Orpheus. He attempted to recover his dead wife, Euridice, from Pluto's realm by putting to sleep the three-headed dog Cerberus, guardian of the entrance to the underworld.

III.1   This scene takes place in a Roman street, paved with stones (lines 29 and 37). It is divided into six episodes: Titus's vain pleas for Quintus and Martius (1–26); his discovery that Lucius is exiled (27–58); his discovery of Lavinia's mutilations (59–149); his sacrifice of his hand to Aaron (150–232); his discovery that he has been tricked (233–86); and the Andronici's commitment to revenge (287–99). The recurrence of the motif of Titus's 'bitter tears' (line 6) emphasizes the crescendo of pathos and grief in this scene. Titus first compares the tears he sheds in vain for Quintus and Martius to the rain which improves the ever-intemperate seasons (16–22). At lines 122–9, Titus invites his family to weep with him over a fountain, which the copious amount of their 'bitter tears' turns into a 'brine pit'. Titus also associates his over-flowing tears with the waters of the river Nile (a river, as line 71 reminds us, that 'disdaineth bounds' in its annual flooding), and finally with the sea (224), before his outburst of laughter at line 263, which marks the lowest point of his despair and the realization that he has 'not another tear to shed' (265).

10   *two-and-twenty* Mutius, though initially disowned, has found his place in the tomb of the Andronici.

13   *languor* corrosive grief

14   *stanch* quench

16   *O earth* Titus's appeal to the earth is more than a one-off gesture; it prepares for the elemental outbursts later in the scene (lines 93–7, 123–9, 210–12 and 220–28).

22   *So* on condition that
      drink . . . blood possible reference to Quintus and Martius's fall into the 'blood-drinking' pit at II.3.224; also a distant echo of Abel's death in Genesis 4:11: 'the earth, which hath opened her mouth to receive thy brother's blood'

24   *reverse the doom of death* suspend the death sentence which is pending over Quintus and Martius's heads. See also lines 47 and 51 below, IV.2.113 and V.3.181.

36   *And . . . them* The Folio conflates this half-line with the next line to read, as in Q3: 'Therefore I tell my sorrowes bootles to the stones.' The Folio version, however, has none of the directness and poignancy of the first two Quartos, where the expected pentameter line, as if overcome by the futility it expresses, fails to complete itself.

40   *intercept* interrupt

43   *grave weeds* solemn dress

44   *afford* provide

45   *soft as wax* proverbial. See *The Rape of Lucrece*, 591–2, where Lucrece pleads with her ravisher to allow her tears to soften his heart 'with their continual motion, | For stones dissolved to water do convert'.

46   *stone is silent* proverbial: 'still as a stone'

54   *wilderness* a place of anarchic lawlessness. See *The Rape of Lucrece*, 543–4: 'a white hind under the gripe's sharp

claws, | Pleads in a wilderness where are no laws'. See also line 94 below.

63   *so she is* The compassionate Marcus has mourned the loss of the unmutilated niece; the realistic Titus asserts his daughter's continued existence in mutilation, as his reproof of Lucius at line 65 indicates.

64   *object* something presented to the sight, as lines 65 and 67 confirm

66–7   *accursèd hand . . . handless* Titus's pun ('accursèd hand' is a synecdoche, 'handless' a literalism) expresses the unnaturalness of what he perceives. He continues later on in this scene to exploit the various applications of the word 'hands', as a symbol of service (lines 73 and 80), and as an instrument of life and of prayer (lines 75–6), until Titus's sacrifice at line 192 reduces the wordplay to grotesque literalism.

68   *What fool . . . sea* proverbial, 'to cast water into the sea'

69   *bright-burning Troy* emblem of terminal conflagration in classical antiquity

70   *grief was at the height* The idea of what constitutes 'the worst' has to be revised three times in the course of this scene: here, then at lines 215–19 and finally at lines 265–86.

72   *I'll chop . . . too* With lines 77–8 and 130 below, this prepares for the actual deed at line 190.

76   *effectless use* useless use, an oxymoron

81   *martyred* mutilated, as at line 107

82   *engine . . . thoughts* Lavinia's tongue

83   *blabbed* prattled, spoke with innocent volubility

84   *pretty hollow cage* Lavinia's mouth

90   *unrecuring* incurable

91   The previous act's imagery of Lavinia as the 'dainty doe' is resumed here, where Titus appropriates Marcus's image of Lavinia as quarry.

93–7   The idea of being swallowed up by elemental nature (II.3.192–245) makes Titus's powerful simile more than a figure of misery: it suggests that as Titus loses faith in *romanitas*, his sense of identity begins to implode.

96   *Expecting ever when* waiting always for the time when *envious* malignant

97   *his* its

101   *spurn* blow

105   *lively* living

107   *martyred* See note to line 81.

109   *by this* by this time

112   *honey-dew* a sweet substance on leaves, originally thought to be distilled like dew

113   *gathered* contracted, and thus forming folds or wrinkles (not 'picked', given the presence of honey-dew). Possibly an attempt on Titus's part to repress the thought that Lavinia has been 'plucked', 'deflowered'.

123   *fountain* water-spring, as at line 127

130   See note to line 72.

131   *dumb shows* those parts of a play representing action without speech. The dramatic conceit is sustained by 'plot' and 'device' (line 134), by the implied audience (line 135), and even by the covert allusion to Kyd's *The Spanish Tragedie* (IV.4.220), where Hieronymo bites out his tongue before killing the Duke of Castile and himself.

140   *napkin* handkerchief

148   *sympathy* community of feeling

149   *limbo is from bliss* Limbo is a region on the border of hell reserved for virtuous pagans and unbaptized infants, debarred from 'bliss' or the joys of paradise (see also line 271). This line cues the entrance of Aaron, who announces 'help' from above (the semi-divine Emperor): but he is a black angel, and the 'ransom' he is about to bring converts 'limbo' into 'hell'. See also next note.

156   *ransom for their fault* This phrase, which traditionally refers to Christ's redeeming sacrifice, feeds Aaron's blasphemous satanism. See also lines 172 ('ransom') and 180 ('redeem').

158   *raven . . . lark* Echoes of Lavinia's proverbial line 'the

raven doth not hatch a lark' at II.3.149 suggest how misplaced Titus's trust in 'gentle Aaron' is.

168–9   *And reared . . . castle* By wielding the battle-axe against the enemy's castle, Titus and Lucius have in effect been 'writing' the public annals of their 'high desert' (line 170) on the stricken ramparts, unlike Marcus, whose hand in this sense has been 'idle' (line 171).

177   *withered herbs* Titus's old hands. Titus has recently used a similar metaphor in relation to Lavinia ('lily almost witherèd', line 113). This time, however, the metaphor prompts the 'plucking up' (line 178) for which his hands are 'meet', that is 'fit'. See note to line 113.

179   *shall* am to

186   *Lend me . . . mine* The word-play is sardonic, not only because of the figurative-literal equivocation on 'hand' (as at line 160), but because of the contrast between the provisional 'lending' and the irrevocable 'giving'.

187   *If . . . honest* If deceit does good, then honesty must be presumed to do evil; thus, if Aaron is to be true to his evil nature, he must be honest. Compare Iago's paradoxical reasoning in *Othello*, II.3.339–53.

189   *in another sort* Aaron discloses his plan at line 201.

190   (stage direction) *left hand* as inferred from a later reference to Titus's right hand (III.2.7)

191   *what shall be is dispatched* what was to be decided (whose hand should be cut off) has already been settled

193   *warded* guarded

195   *that* i.e. burial

200   *Look . . . to* expect

202   *fat* feed succulently

206   *ruin* a body decayed as well as mutilated

210   *breathe . . . dim* obscure the sky, as a glass is misted by breath

213   *with* within the bounds of. Marcus's rational resistance to hyperbole prepares for the shock of his about-turn at line 240.

215   *Is . . . sorrows* See note to II.3.13.

219   *bind* confine

220   *o'erflow* become flooded

221   *sea wax mad* proverbial, 'as mad as the troubled sea'

222   *welkin* sky

223   *coil* commotion

224–5   *I am . . . earth* Lavinia with her sighs and tears is the sky
      with its wind and rain; Titus in his responsiveness to
      her is the flooded earth and the tempestuous sea. The
      chiasmus (an AB:BA sequence) is obscured, but not
      abolished, by the stop after 'sea'.

229–32   *For why . . . tongues.* The modulation of the simile from
      flooding (through too much rain) to vomiting (through
      too much drinking) displays the convulsive, uncontrol-
      lable interdependence of Titus's grief and its expression.

231–2   *losers . . . tongues* proverbial, 'give losers leave to speak'.
      Compare *2 Henry VI*, III.1.182: 'But I can give the loser
      leave to chide.'

237–9   *Thy grief . . . death.* The messenger's sympathetic
      response to Titus's plight represents the first indication
      that popular feeling in Rome will turn against the
      Emperor and his allies.

240   *hot Etna* an active volcano in Sicily

243   *To weep . . . weep* biblical: 'Weep with them that weep'
      (Romans 12:15)

244   *flouted at* mocked

247   *bear his name* still be called life

250   *starvèd* numbed through cold, and certainly not to be
      revived by 'frozen water'. In *2 Henry VI*, III.1.343, York
      warns the nobles not to 'warm the starvèd snake'.

251   *When . . . end?* See also II.4.13–15.

252   *flatt'ry* illusory comfort

255   *dear* grievous

258   *control* restrain

259–60   *thy other hand . . . teeth* This prepares for line 281.

261   *The closing . . . eyes* let this sight be the last thing we see

263   *Ha, ha, ha!* Laughter as a symptom of crazed grief is
      anticipated in Kyd's *The Spanish Tragedie*, III.11.77–8.

268   *tributary* See note to I.1.162.

269   *cave* The lair of Revenge, like that of other personifications of primitive instinct, is placed beyond the frontiers of human society.

271   *bliss* See note to line 149.

272   *returned again* avenged

275   *heavy* sorrowing

280–81   *Lavinia . . . thy teeth* Possibly prompted by lines 259–60. See Introduction, p. 49.

284   *Hie* go quickly

290   *pledges* his promises, but also his family, the persons to whom he is pledged by kinship and whose love will guarantee his return

292   *tofore* formerly

297   *Tarquin and his queen* See note to II.1.108.

III.2   This scene is first found in the First Folio, and is believed to represent a later addition to the original play as preserved by the First Quarto. See An Account of the Text, p. 230. The location is Titus's house.

4   *sorrow-wreathen knot* arms folded out of sorrow

6   *passionate* express passion fittingly

12   *map* model, or emblem

15   *Wound . . . groans* Sighing and groaning were thought to drain the heart of blood.

16–17   *little knife . . . hole* Compare *Richard II*, III.2.169–70: 'with a little pin | Bores through his castle wall, and farewell, king!'

19   *sink* receptacle for liquid

20   *fool* a term of compassionate tenderness

23   *dote* talk like a madman

25   *What . . . life?* Titus's punning continues the regression from metaphor to literalism which started in the previous scene. See note to III.1.66–7.

27–8   *Aeneas . . . miserable* In Virgil's *Aeneid* II.2, Aeneas begins his narration of the fall of Troy with the words:

'O Queen, you require me to revive unutterable grief.'

29   *handle ... hands* Titus's obsessive punning shows that *he* cannot forget his and Lavinia's mutilations, as he himself goes on to recognize at lines 32–3.

31   *square* shape

35–6   *Here ... signs* Titus, who has to help her to eat, finds her goblet empty, but is informed by her, maybe by a shake of the head, that she does not want to drink.

38   *mashed* fermented, a technical term from beer-making, developing 'brewed'. This metaphor reminds us that in the polluted Elizabethan cities a 'drink' was not water but beer.

40   *perfect* as in 'word-perfect'

41   *begging hermits* religious mendicants

45   *still* continuous

55   *cloyed* satiated with excess

62   *lamenting doings* helpless meanderings

66   *ill-favoured* ugly

71   *insult on* triumph over

72   *Flattering ... as if* deceiving myself with the thought that

80   *shadows for true substances* proverbial

81   *take away* clear the table

82   *closet* private room

82–3   *read ... of old* For the nostalgia of impotence, compare *Richard II*, III.2.155–6: 'let us sit upon the ground | And tell sad stories of the death of kings', or *King Lear*, V.3.8–19.

85   *dazzle* lose the faculty of distinct and steady vision, usually from ageing

IV.1   The location of this scene is the atrium, or inner court, of Titus's house. The action is divided into two episodes: the identification of Lavinia's assailants (1–79) and the diverse reactions to the discovery (80–130).

9   *somewhat* something

10–15   The First Quarto gives to Titus lines 9–15. Some of
         these lines must be attributed to Marcus, for lines 18–
         19 indicate that Young Lucius is answering his uncle,
         not his grandfather. The question is where to restore the
         dropped speech prefix MARCUS. Line 10 commends itself
         because of the repetition of 'Lucius' from line 9.

12   *Cornelia* Daughter of Scipio Africanus, Roman con-
         queror of Carthage, and mother of the Gracchi brothers,
         she is probably the most famous of the Roman matrons.

13   *Read to* instructed

14   *Sweet poetry* Possibly this is Ovid's poetry, should Shake-
         speare have the Grammar School curriculum in mind.

         Tully's Orator Marcus Tullius Cicero was formally
         known in the Renaissance as Tully. The book referred
         to could be either his *Orator ad M. Brutum*, a sketch of
         the ideal orator, or his *De Oratore*, a treatise on rhetoric.

15   *plies* importunes

20   *Hecuba of Troy* See note to I.1.139–41.

24   *but in fury* except in a fit of frenzy

26   *Causeless* without good reason

27   *go* go with me

28   *attend* wait upon

39   *fact* crime

41   *tosseth* throws to and fro

42   *Ovid's Metamorphoses* This most famous of compilations,
         perhaps the most influential classical text on the art and
         literature of the Renaissance, was available to Shake-
         speare in Arthur Golding's 1585–7 translation, as well
         as in the original Latin.

44   *culled* picked out

47–8   *Philomel . . . rape* Tereus is guilty of 'treason' because he
         betrays the trust not only of Pandion, the King of Athens
         and his father-in-law, but also of Procne his wife, and
         most of all of Philomela, his sister-in-law.

49   *annoy* grievous injury

50   *quotes* scrutinizes

51   *surprised* seized suddenly, as at I.1.287

53   *forced* raped

56   *Patterned by that* Titus implies that Nature is imitating Art and that because Lavinia's 'actual' rape possesses the completeness of Ovid's 'artistic' representation of Philomela's rape, her plight belongs to the realm of the tragic.

59   *tragedies* human suffering (but also a metadramatic allusion to the delight audiences take in watching tragedies)

62–3   *Tarquin . . . Lucrece* See note to II.1.108.

65   *Apollo, Pallas, Jove or Mercury* Apollo was the divinity of law, Pallas Athene was the goddess of wisdom and war, Jove was the guardian of justice and virtue, and Mercury was the god of cunning and prudence. These attributes all bear upon the crime about to be revealed.

68   *plain* level

71   *shift* expedient

73   *will have discovered for revenge* wishes to have revealed so that it may be avenged. The pious Marcus anachronistically seeks to reconcile the divine injunction against revenge – 'Vengeance is mine; I will repay, saith the Lord' (Romans, 12:19) – with the secular need for retribution. See also lines 127–8 below.

74   *plain* legibly

77   *Stuprum* (Latin) rape

80–81 *Magni . . . vides?* (Latin) 'master of the great heavens [i.e. Jove or Zeus], do you so calmly [*tam lentus*] hear crimes, so calmly see them?', from Seneca's *Hippolytus*, 671–2

85   *exclaims* outcries

87   *Roman Hector* Lucius, champion of Rome, as Hector was champion of Troy.

88   *fere* husband

90   *Junius Brutus* the Roman patriot who persuaded Collatine, Lucrece's husband, to avenge her, and who led the revolt against the Tarquins. See *The Rape of Lucrece*, 1807–34.

91   *good advice* careful deliberation

93   *reproach* dishonour

94   *and* if

95   *bear-whelps* Chiron and Demetrius. Similarly 'dam' at
        line 96 is Tamora and 'lion' at line 97 Saturninus.

96   *wind* scent

98–9   *And lulls . . . list* By yielding to Saturninus sexually
        ('playeth on her back') Tamora gets him to yield to her
        politically ('do what she list'). The contrast is between a
        sleeping lion, and a wakeful she-bear who has Rome at
        her mercy.

100   *young huntsman* inexperienced as a hunter
        Let alone leave it alone

101   *leaf* sheet, but also 'foliage', thus anticipating line 107

102   *gad* spike used for engraving
        these words the words written by Lavinia

104   *Sybil's leaves* The prophecies of the Sybil at Cuma were
        written on leaves that sometimes blew away before they
        could be collected. See Virgil, *Aeneid* VI.74–5: 'Only
        trust not thy verses to leaves, lest they fly in disorder,
        the sport of rushing winds.' Like the leaves, the 'sands'
        contain a supreme but very vulnerable 'lesson' (line 105).

110   *done the like* defended Rome from foreign invaders

113   *fit* equip. An echo of Hieronymo's famous phrase, 'Why
        then Ile fit you', which launches his revenge, in Kyd's
        The Spanish Tragedie, IV.1.68.

120   *brave it* swagger

121   *waited on* not ignored, as they have been up to now

123   *compassion* take pity on

124   *ecstasy* mad fits

128   *Revenge the heavens* let the heavens take revenge

IV.2   The setting is a room in the Imperial Palace. The action
        comprises the reception of Titus's gifts (1–31); the reac-
        tion to the news that Tamora has a son (32–50); the
        Nurse's presentation of his black son to Aaron for dis-
        patching (51–82); Aaron's protection of his child from

Demetrius and Chiron (83–126); Aaron's arrangements to secure the child's survival and to protect the Empress's good name, which involve the brutal murder of the Nurse (127–70); and his decision to entrust the child to the Goths (171–9).

0   (stage direction) *another* An attendant is required to carry the 'presents' referred to in IV.1.113–15.

6   *confound* destroy. Young Lucius's three asides, here and at lines 8–9 and 17, sustain the boyish bravado that surfaced at IV.1.106–8.

7   *Gramercy* thank you. The tone is patronizingly courtly.

8   *deciphered* detected, by means of reading

10   *well advised* acting rationally. Lucius is contradicting Aaron at line 3, but without betraying himself.

16   *appointed* equipped with weapons

18   *round about* all round

20–21 *Integer . . . arcu* (Latin) from Horace, *Odes*, I.22.1–2: '[The man] upright of life and unstained by crime does not need the javelins or the bow of the Moor.'

23   *grammar* Lily's *Latin Grammar*, the prescribed textbook in late sixteenth-century grammar schools, quotes these lines twice.

24   *just* precisely. Aaron spots at once the ironic applicability of the quotation to Lavinia's rapists.

25   *ass* the standard epithet for the class-room dunce

26   *no sound jest* no honest joke. Aaron understands the real meaning of Titus's gesture, which is far from conciliatory.

28   *wound . . . quick* proverbial, 'to wound to the quick', the 'quick' being acutely sensitive parts of the body

30   *conceit* clever idea, that is Titus's jest at line 26

31   *let her . . . awhile* Tamora is in labour, as anticipated at line 29 and confirmed at line 47. For the phrasing, see note to II.3.8. This birth is an early example of Shakespearean double-time: the momentum of the play's events makes improbable the nine months required since Tamora's marriage to Saturninus, whom Rome believes

to be the father of the child; yet the required period is rendered plausible by the slow maturing of Titus's madness and revenge, and of Lucius's ascendancy over the Gothic army.

32–6   *And now . . . hearing* Aaron's defiance of Marcus in the hearing of Titus has not been shown.

38   *insinuate* curry favour

40   *friendly* This prompts a running blaspheming gag – 'charitable' (43), 'full of love' (43), 'amen' (44), 'pray' (46), 'belovèd' (47) – which is nailed by Aaron at line 48.

42   *At such a bay* so brought to bay, a resumption of the hunting analogy first introduced in Act II
      by turn in turn, but also by the sexual act. See note to II.1.96.

43   Chiron's blasphemous joke turns on the ambiguity of the word 'love', which can mean either 'charity' (in the Christian sense) or 'lust'.

45   *more* in addition to the 'thousand Roman dames' at line 41

46   *pray* The sons' cynicism seems to turn sentimental as soon as their mother is involved. Their inconsistency rightly earns Aaron's contempt at line 48.

50   *Belike* possibly

53   *more . . . whit* Aaron's sardonic puns on more/Moor and whit/white prepare for the Nurse's disclosure, when his name and skin-colour abruptly cease to be a joke.

62   *To whom* Aaron affects to take the Nurse's 'is delivered' to mean 'has been handed over' and not 'has given birth'.

63   *good rest* further wilful misunderstanding

67   *as . . . toad* proverbial

71   *Zounds* The Folio dilutes the expletive 'Zounds', derived from 'God's wounds', to 'Out you', because of the Profanity Act against blasphemy (1606).

72   *blowze* ruddy-faced girl, provocatively applied to Aaron's black baby

75   *undone* ruin the reputation of

76   *done* had sex with

82–3   *let . . . blood* Aaron claims the same paternal privilege of life and death over his son as Titus does in Act I.

84   *broach* pierce, as with a spit
        rapier light fencing sword

88–9   *burning . . . was got* Here 'burning' suggests both the sexual fierceness of the occasion and the potency of the pagan divinities Aaron invokes.

92   *Enceladus* one of the legendary Titans who attacked the Olympians and ignited the volcano of Etna

93   *Typhon* monstrous giant who nearly destroyed Olympus

94   *Alcides* Hercules
        god of war Mars

95   *seize this prey* The hunting metaphor is resumed again here. See note to line 42.

96   *sanguine* red-faced. Aaron introduces the motif of the superiority of black complexion over white (or ruddy), which he then develops at length at lines 97–102 and 115–18.
        shallow-hearted superficially valiant

97   *white-limed* whitewashed, punning on 'white-limbed', as suggested by the original spelling in Q2–3 'white limbde' and F1–2 'white-limb'd'.
        alehouse painted signs Public-house signs were notorious for the crudeness of the drawing. See, for example, *2 Henry VI*, III.2.80–81: 'Erect his statue and worship it, | And make my image but an alehouse sign.'

98–9   *Coal-black . . . hue* proverbial, 'black will take no other hue'

100–101 *For . . . white* proverbial, 'to wash a blackamoor (Ethiope) white'

102   *lave* wash

104   *excuse it* account for the baby's complexion

107   *vigour . . . picture* life and form. Compare V.1.45, where Lucius captures both attributes in the phrase 'growing image'.

109   *maugre* in spite of

110   *smoke* burn

112   *escape* escapade

113   *doom* See note to III.1.24.

114   *ignomy* ignominy

117   *close enacts* secret resolutions

118   *leer* countenance

121   *sensibly* feelingly, perceptibly or made capable of sensation. Combined with 'fed', however, 'sensibly' is merely a reinforcement of 'gave life' in the next line, and should not be attributed with over-specific meanings other than 'nourished' or 'sustained'.

123   *womb . . . imprisoned* A distant echo of the 'loathsome pit' in II.3, described there as a 'swallowing womb' at line 239 and 'subtle hole' at line 198. See head-note to II.3.

124   *enfranchisèd* freed

125   *the surer side* proverbial

126   *seal* Aaron's complexion, hence his paternity

129   *subscribe to* acquiesce in

132   *have . . . you* a further development of the hunting metaphor resumed from lines 42 and 95

137   *chafèd* enraged

143   *Two . . . away* proverbial

145   *Wheak* mimetic term, the Elizabethan equivalent of 'squeak'

147   *policy* realistic statecraft, a term associated with the Machiavellian villain. See notes to II.1.104 and 123.

149   *babbling gossip* Compare with 'babbling fountain' at II.4.23.

151   *Muly lives* 'Muliteus', the alternative reading preserved in Q and F1 is likely to be a corruption of the reading adopted in this edition, as 'Muly', a well-known Moorish name, rather than a pseudo-Latin name, such as 'Muliteus', seems appropriate for Aaron's 'countryman'. Besides, 'Muliteus' is syntactically awkward in the context of lines 151–3 and 'leus' can be easily explained as a misreading of 'lives'.

154   *pack* come to an arrangement. The register is contemptuous.

155   *circumstance* details

159   *tempest* scandal, should the identity of Tamora's baby be discovered

161   *physic* medicine. The register is brutally ironic.

162   *bestow* provide. The funeral in question will be no more genuine than Aaron's 'physic'.

163   *grooms* manual servants

164   *days* time

165   *presently* at once

167   *tattle* chatter emptily, as gossip can do him no harm, once all witnesses have been dispatched

168   *trust the air* proverbial

171   *as swift . . . flies* proverbial. See note to II.2.24.

172   *dispose* put away safely

173   *secretly . . . friends* Aaron is unaware that the Goths are now supporting Lucius's cause.

175   *puts . . . shifts* proverbial, 'makes us devise stratagems'

176–7 *feed . . . curds* The First Quarto's repetition of 'feed' seems appropriate, indeed expressive. Aaron's unself-conscious paternal pride has, in the rhythm and syntax so preserved, a touching simplicity.

178   *cabin* lodge (verb)

IV.3   This scene is located outside the Imperial Palace. It consists of the lament for Justice (1–49), the allegorical archery-shoot (50–76), and the enrolment of the clown as messenger (77–119). It develops Titus's counterplot from the first section of the previous scene.

0   (stage direction) *his son Publius* For Publius's relation to Marcus, see line 26.

2   *your archery* arrows bearing a hostile note

3   *draw home enough* stretch the bow sufficiently to ensure that the arrow strikes home

4   *Terras Astraea reliquit* (Latin) from Ovid, *Metamorphoses* I.150: 'Astraea [the goddess of justice] has left the earth'. The departure of Justice announces the arrival of the age

of iron, the fourth and final stage of the world's decline
from an original golden age.

8   *Happily* by good fortune

11   *mattock* heavy tool used for digging up hard ground. A
famous precedent of the motif of digging the earth to
find justice is in Thomas Kyd, *The Spanish Tragedie*
(IV.12.71): 'Away, Ile rip the bowels of the earth, (*He
diggeth with his Dagger.*)'

13   *Pluto* Roman god of the underworld, also at line 38

18–20   *Ah, Rome . . . o'er me* Titus accepts political responsibility
for the disappearance of Justice in Rome.

19   *What time* when

22   *man-of-war* fighting ship, anticipating 'shipped' in the
next line. Titus casts his kinsmen as customs officers.

24   *pipe* whistle for, thus completing the sequence of nautical
images

29   *feed his humour* proverbial, 'co-operate with his whims'.
Compare *Richard III*, IV.1.64: 'To feed my humour
wish thyself no harm', and *King Lear*, IV.1.40–41: 'Bad
is the trade that must play fool to sorrow, | Ang'ring
itself and others.'

32   *But* The catchword at the foot of the page of the First
Quarto ('But') is followed by a different word at the top
of the next page ('Ioine'). It is possible that one line, or
even two, may have been omitted.

34   *wreak* revenge

37   *her* Astraea. See note to line 4 above.

42   *stay a time* wait a while

43   *feed . . . delays* proverbial

44   *burning lake* standard name for Phlegethon, one of the
four rivers of the underworld. It is anticipated by Kyd
in *The Spanish Tragedie*, III.12.11: 'That leades unto the
lake where hell doth stand.'

45   *her* Revenge or Justice. The ambiguity is significant.
Acheron another underworld river, round which the
shades of the dead hover, including the shade of Revenge

46   *shrubs . . . cedars* proverbial, 'high cedars fall when low shrubs remain'

47   *Cyclops* one-eyed giants who devoured human beings. See, for example, Homer, *Odyssey* IX.

48   *steel . . . back* proverbial, 'he is steel to the back'

53   *to this gear* to the business

54–5   *Ad Jovem . . . Ad Apollinem . . . Ad Martem* (Latin) to Jove . . . to Apollo . . . to Mars

58   *were as good* might as well

60   *Of* on

64   *well said* good shot

65   *Virgo* zodiacal constellation of the Virgin, identified with the figure of Justice. However, the obscene connotations reactivated at line 69 encourage an ironic association of Virgo with Tamora.

69   *Taurus* zodiacal constellation of the Bull. Horns are the signs of cuckoldry: in Titus's less-than-fantastic allegory, the misconduct of the Virgo (Tamora) is related to the horns of Taurus (Saturninus).

71   *Aries* zodiacal constellation of the Ram. Marcus elaborates Titus's allegory on the basis that the Ram and the Bull are neighbouring constellations, and that Saturninus has been cuckolded by Aaron.

76   *God . . . joy* traditional blessing for newly weds. This ends the vein of erotic mockery opened at line 65.

76   *News . . . come* line erroneously assigned to Clown in Q1

80   *gibbet-maker* The Quarto spells Jupiter 'Iubiter' at lines 67, 79, 83 and 84, perhaps to underline the pun for its readers. The Clown understands 'gibbeter' (= maker of gibbets), prompting the retention of the spelling 'Jubiter' at line 84 in this edition.

81   *them* the gallows

90   *press* hasten

92   *tribunal plebs* malapropism for *tribunus plebis*, or 'tribune of the people'

       take up settle

93   *Emperal* malapropism for 'Emperor'

95   *oration* petition

98   *with a grace* gracefully, but the Clown wilfully takes it to mean 'with a thanks to God for food'

106–13 *Sirrah . . . Let me alone* See An Account of the Text, p. 231.

116   *For thou must hold it* This conjectural emendation is preferable to the original in Q and F ('For thou hast made it'), as Titus is more likely to be addressing the Clown, as suggested by the pronoun 'thou', which Titus never uses to address Marcus.

IV.4   This scene is located in the state-room of the Imperial Palace. It dramatizes the emperor's rage at Titus's provocative behaviour (lines 1–38); the summary execution of the clown (lines 39–60); and the news of Lucius's approach with an army of Goths, followed by Tamora's proposed counter to that threat (lines 61–112).

2   *overborne* oppressed

3   *extent* exercise

4   *egall* impartial, from 'equal to all', a legal term from Norman French. See also *The Merchant of Venice*, III.4.13: 'an egall yoke of love'.

6–7   *However . . . ears* despite the accusations the Andronici have publicly levelled against him

8   *even* level, in accord

11   *wreaks* vindictive actions

16   *Sweet* ironic, in fact, most unwelcome

18   *blazoning* loudly proclaiming

19   *humour* caprice

21   *ecstasies* See note to IV.1.124.

23–6 *justice . . . that lives* Compare *Measure for Measure*, II.2.90: 'The law hath not been dead, though it hath slept.'

35   *gloze with all* flatter everybody, notably Saturninus at lines 27–8, and Titus's supporters at lines 32–4. But Tamora's satisfaction at her own cleverness ('High-

216

witted') is misplaced. She is wrong in her claim that Titus is helplessly deranged (line 31), and in her reliance on Aaron's manipulations (lines 37–8).

36   *touched* wounded. See note to IV.2.28.

37   *out* having been drawn out

42   *Saint Stephen* the first martyr stoned to death outside Jerusalem

48   *by'Lady* by our Lady (the Virgin Mary), but also 'by (the command of) a lady'; hence the pun on 'fair end' and 'an end set by the fair sex'

57   *shape privilege* create immunity

58   *slaughterman* executioner

63   *gathered head* raised an army

64   *bent . . . spoil* intent on pillage

65   *amain* with all speed

68   *Coriolanus* The military defender of the early Roman Republic who, having been banished, marched on Rome at the head of her enemies, threatening to burn her. Shakespeare dramatizes the story in *Coriolanus*, the last of his plays to be based closely on Roman history.

70   *nip* to pinch off the buds or shoots of a plant; hence to 'hang the head', and the similes at line 71

75   *walkèd . . . man* This is a reference to the often dramatized practice, whereby the ruler visits his subjects incognito in order to gather intelligence and unmask corruption, as in Shakespeare's *Measure for Measure* or Thomas Middleton's *The Phoenix*, and/or to strengthen the bond with his people, as in Shakespeare's *Henry V* or the anonymous *Fair Em* (*c.* 1590).

76   *wrongfully* wrongfully ordered

84   *is not careful* does not care

86   *stint* stop

87   *giddy* fickle, without principles

89   *enchant* bewitch

91   *honey-stalks* clover stalks, a surfeit of which can be fatal to sheep

92   *When as* when
96   *smooth* flatter
105   *stand in* insist on
109   *temper* mould or shape
113   *incessantly* immediately

V.1   The location is in the country on the approaches to
      Rome. The scene, framed by two brief episodes of politi-
      cal action focusing on the Goths' support of Lucius (1–
      18) and on Lucius's acceptance of Saturninus's invitation
      to attend a parley in Rome (152–65), is taken up with
      the capture of Aaron and the 'irreligious' confession of
      his crimes against the Andronici (19–151).
1   *Approvèd* tested
7   *scath* injury
9   *slip* shoot or twig of a branch, hence heir
13   *bold* confident
15   *master* In Elizabethan times, the bee-hive was thought to
      be ruled by a king-bee. See *Henry V*, I.2.190: 'They
      [honey bees] have a king . . . of sorts'.
16   *cursèd Tamora* Tamora, sharing 'ingrateful' Rome's
      indifference (line 12) to Titus's military feats, is now
      considered an enemy by the 'warlike' Goth, who is aware
      of his own switch of allegiance (see line 10).
19   *lusty* strong, vigorous
21   *ruinous monastery* A reference to the state of the English
      monasteries after the Reformation, with their 'Bare
      ruined choirs' (Sonnet 73.4), would reinforce their
      attraction to fugitives like Aaron, and to 'earnest' con-
      templatives like the Goth.
22   *earnestly* steadfastly
26   *controlled* See note to III.1.258.
27   *tawny* black
28   *bewray* discover unintentionally
33   *rates* scolds
39   *use . . . of* deal . . . with

42   *pearl ... eye* proverbial, 'a black man is a pearl in a fair woman's eye'

44   *wall-eyed* glaring-eyed. Compare *King John*, IV.3.49: 'wall-eyed wrath or staring rage'.

50   *sire* father

51   *sprawl* twitch limbs convulsively

55   *show* reveal to

60   *nourished* 'cared for', as well as 'fed'

65   *Complots* Aaron's self-fashioning as author of tragic (com)plots is suggestively metadramatic. See also note to IV.1.59.

66   *Ruthful ... piteously performed* pitiful ... performed in order to provoke pity

71–2 *Who ... oath?* In his *Arte of War* (translated by Peter Whithorn: 2nd edn, 1588), Machiavelli raises this very dilemma when discussing mercenaries: 'By what God or by what saints may I make them to swear? By those that they worship, or by those that they blaspheme? Who they worship I know not any: but I know well they blaspheme all. How shall I believe that they will keep their promise to them, whom every hour they despise?' See Further Reading, Maxwell, p. 104.

74   *for* because

76   *popish ... ceremonies* To a Protestant audience this should evoke 'superstitious ceremonies'; but given that a criminal atheist is speaking, audience response is likely to have been more complex.

79   *bauble* jester's baton

88   *luxurious* lustful

90   *To* compared with

93   *trimmed* tidied by removing overgrowth, but also copulated with

95   *washed ... trimmed* as by a barber

96   *Trim sport* fine or excellent entertainment. Aaron's brutal punning proliferates.

99   *codding* lustful

100   *As sure ... set* proverbial, 'without doubt'

102   *at head* The best bull-dogs attacked the bull head-on.

103   *worth* Aaron's merits as a tutor

104   *trained* enticed

110   *stroke of mischief* harmful part

113   *broke my heart* died. Aaron is referring to III.1.201–4.

114   *pried me* spied on me

119   *sounded* swooned

122   *like a black dog* proverbial, 'to blush like a black dog'.
        Compare with IV.2.115–17.

125–7   *Even . . . notorious ill* Compare *The Troublesome Reign of
        King John* (1591): 'How, what, when and where, have I
        bestow'd a day | That tended not to some notorious ill?'
        (Part II, 8. 85–6).

126   *Few* few days

128–40 *As kill . . . dead* This boastful catalogue is a variation of
        Barabas's list in Marlowe's *Jew of Malta*, II.3.176–202.

142   *kill a fly* This passing remark may have prompted the
        climax of III.2, the so-called 'fly killing scene', which
        was added later.

146   *presently* immediately

149   *So* as long as

160   *Willing you* bidding you

V.2   The location is the atrium of Titus's house, with his
        study represented by the upper stage. The scene com-
        prises Tamora's entrance into Titus's property (1–8);
        her success in persuading Titus to come down to her
        (9–69); her briefing of her sons about her intentions
        (70–80); her success in getting Titus and Marcus to
        invite Lucius and the Gothic chiefs to a feast with
        Saturninus and his entourage (91–131); her consent to
        her sons' remaining with Titus (132–48); their arrest by
        Titus's men (149–64); and Titus's statement of what
        will happen to them and why, ending with his cutting
        their throats (165–204).

1   *sad habiliment* dismal costume. Tamora is dressed as a

personification of Revenge, as indicated in the opening stage direction.

3   *from below* Compare with IV.3.11–14 and 44–5.

8   *confusion* ruin

9   *Who . . . contemplation?* J. C. Maxwell (see Further Reading) points out that this famous entry-line is comically remembered by the clown at line 1963 in Thomas Dekker's *The Welsh Embassador* (Malone Society Reprints, ed. H. Littledale and W. W. Greg, 1921). This play provides further evidence of popular response to *Titus Andronicus*: line 976 repeats Shakespeare's 'leaf of brass' (IV.1.101). Given that *The Welsh Embassador* can safely be dated at 1623 (line 2162 refers to 'yeares 1621'), it bears witness to the remarkable longevity of Shakespeare's tragedy for the play-going public of the period.

11   *sad . . . away* solemn resolutions may be scattered by the wind Titus continues to harp on the vulnerability of his vengeance, as at IV.1.103–5.

14   *bloody lines* written in blood. See also 'crimson lines' at line 22 below.

18   *Wanting . . . action?* lacking a hand with which to dramatize my speech. Conjectural emendation of the corrupt reading preserved in Q ('Wanting a hand to give it that accord'), supported by a detail in 'The Ant and the Nightingale', where Thomas Middleton has a mutilated soldier referring to 'my lamentable action of one arm, like old *Titus Andronicus*' (*The Works of Thomas Middleton*, 8 vols., London, 1885–6, ed. A. H. Bullen, vol. 8, p. 94).

19   *odds of* advantage over

22–5   *Witness* The cumulative repetition of this word is a forensic device much used in the drama that preceded *Titus*, such as *Locrine* (1591–5) V.1.11–12 and *Selimus* (*c.* 1591), lines 1476–86.

23   *trenches* deep wrinkles

30   *th'infernal kingdom* Hades, the underworld realm of Pluto

31   *gnawing vulture* The metaphor is from Prometheus's vulture. See note to II.1.17.

32   *wreakful vengeance* a pleonasm: 'revengeful revenge'

38   *couch* lie hidden, lurk

45   *Rape and Murder* Titus has identified their alleged identities by means of the allegorical 'habiliments' noted in the opening stage direction.

      stands See note to II.3.13.

46   *surance* guarantee

47   *chariot wheels* Titus's reference to Revenge's chariot should not be regarded as an implied stage direction. For similar examples, see I.1.252.

50   *proper* handsome

51   hale *haul*

56   *Hyperion* the sun-god, who, like Revenge, girdles the globe, but in a golden chariot drawn by white steeds

59   *So* provided that

60   *ministers* administrators

65   *worldly* mortal, of this world

70   *closing* agreeing

71   *forge* invent

76   *sure* under control

77   *practice out of hand* improvised expedient

78   *giddy* See note to IV.4.87.

80   *ply my theme* work assiduously at my plan

82   *Fury* one of the Eumenides or avenging deities

85   *Well . . . fitted . . . Moor* you would be perfectly equipped were you supplied with a Moor

87   *wags* moves about

89   *represent* act as or depict

90   *convenient* in keeping

101   *hap* luck

107   *up and down* exactly, completely

112   *thrice-valiant* See note to I.1.123.

120   *device* contrivance. See also III.1.131.

124   *repair* return

129   *let him* let him do

136   *cleave* cling. Titus cunningly threatens to take his

revenge out of Tamora's hands and leave it to Lucius
and his army.

139   *governed . . . jest* handled the joke we have planned

140   *smooth . . . him fair* flatter and humour him

141   *turn again* return

143   *And will . . . devices* and will beat them at their own game.
See also III.1.131 and line 120.

147   *complot* covert design planned in concert. See also V.1.65
and note.

156   *therefore* for that reason, since their names describe their
deeds
gentle well-born

159   *sure* securely

160   *cry* cry out

162   (stage direction) *Publius . . . Demetrius* Aaron, Chiron
and Demetrius, the three characters who connived to
mutilate Lavinia's tongue, are now gagged. The brutal
logic of Titus's revenge starts to unfold.

169   *Here stands . . . mud* See *The Rape of Lucrece*, line 577:
'Mud not the fountain that gave drink to thee'.

179   *martyr* slay cruelly

187   *coffin* burial case for a corpse, but also mould of paste for
a pie

188   *pasties* meat-pies

190   *Like . . . increase.* The earth as devourer of its own
offspring is a recurrent motif in the play. See, for
example, III.1.16–22.

193–4   *Philomel . . . Procne* Compare Seneca's *Thyestes* (lines
272–8): 'Tereus' Thracian house saw an abominable
banquet. I concede, it was a monstrous crime; but it is
one that has already been performed. My anguish must
devise something better than that. Inspire my soul, O
Daulian mother and sister [namely, Procne and Philo-
mela]; my case is like yours; help and urge on my hand.
Let the joyful and greedy father tear his sons to pieces
and devour his own flesh.' For Shakespeare's use of his

main source in Ovid's *Metamorphoses*, see Introduction, pp. 13–14.

198   *temper* mix

200   *officious* diligently busy

202   *Centaurs' feast* Perithous, King of the Lapiths, a mythical people from Thessaly, invited the Centaurs (creatures with the head, arms and torso of a man, and the body and legs of a horse) to his wedding feast, at which a bloody fight ensued.

204   *against* by the time that

V.3   The location is as for V.2. This scene is divided into two parts: the end of the old regime (1–65) and the birth of the new (66–198). The first part comprises the arrival and reception of Lucius and the Goths in Rome (1–25), Titus's presentation of his feast, with the killings of Lavinia, Tamora, Titus and Saturninus (26–65). The second part consists firstly of Marcus and Lucius's speeches of exculpation and explanation to the Roman people, and Lucius's election as Emperor (66–147). It then concludes with the contrasting treatments of the dead Romans (Lavinia, Titus, and even Saturninus), and of the dead Tamora and still living Aaron (148–98).

3   *ours with thine* our mind is at one with yours, following 'my father's mind' in line 1.

4   *in* into Titus's house

9   *our friends* either the Gothic allies whom Lucius has brought into Rome with him, or Roman supporters. Lucius is not helplessly delivering himself into Saturninus's hands.

13   *venomous . . . swelling heart* See also *Arden of Feversham* (I.327): 'the rancorous venom of thy mis-swollen heart', George Peele's *The Battle of Alcazar* (II.3.3): 'The fatal poison of my swelling heart', and Shakespeare's near-contemporary *1 Henry VI* (III.1.26): 'From envious malice of thy swelling heart'.

14   *unhallowed* unblessed, profane

16   (stage direction) *Exeunt Goths* The 'chiefest princes of
       the Goths' remain (V.2.125).

17   *more suns than one* Saturninus recognizes Lucius as a
       rival to the throne. See IV.4.77.

18   *What boots it thee* what use is it to you

19   *break the parle* open the parley

21   *careful* painstaking, but also full of grief

28   *cheer be poor* the fare be simple. A pasty occupied a
       modest place in Elizabethan standards of hospitality.

35   *resolve me this* settle this (doubtful point) for me

36   *Virginius* The story of Virginius's killing of his daughter
       Virginia is told by Livy in his history of the foundation
       of Roman institutions, *History of Rome* III, 44–9 (see *The
       Early History of Rome, Books I–IV*, Penguin Classics,
       translated by Aubrey de Selincourt, 1997, pp. 215–21).
       Appius Claudius, the most powerful of the *decemviri* (a
       group of ten magistrates with supreme power to establish
       the legal codes of Rome in 450 BC), made plans to ravish
       Lavinia. To forestall this fate, her father, a humble but
       respected military officer, killed her. This principled
       outrage prompted a revolution against the *decemviri*, and
       when Appius was eventually summoned to appear before
       the Roman tribunal he took his own life.

43   *pattern* model
       lively warrant vivid, forcible authorization

47   *unkind* See note to I.1.89.

48   *tears . . . blind* This brings to a climax a paradox linking
       paternal grief and blindness introduced by Marcus at
       II.4.52–3 and developed by Titus at III.1.268.

58   *presently* at once

60   *daintily* fastidiously. Compare *Tamburlaine* Part I,
       IV.4.24–5: 'Are you so daintily brought up you cannot
       eat your own flesh?'

62   *witness . . . point* The proof that Tamora is guilty of
       eating her own sons is her execution for that crime.

65   *meed for meed* proverbial

67–8   *By uproars . . . gusts* the commotion on stage, but also the disintegration of civil life under Saturninus

70   *scattered . . . sheaf* a strewn harvest, reassembled into an ordered stook. This is an agrarian version of the idea of the 'body politic', which appears in the next line.

71–2   *body, | Lest* The first Quarto assigns lines 72–92 to a 'Roman Lord', the First Folio to a 'Goth'. Both begin this new speech with a variant sentence: 'Let Rome herself . . .' The Folio solution can be rejected with confidence: not even an incompetent playwright would assign lines 79–86 to a non-Roman. Yet the Folio intervention is significant, in that it registers dissatisfaction with the Quarto text. It is therefore reasonable to assume that the compositor of the Quarto introduced the speech prefix 'Roman Lord' on his own initiative, maybe on the basis of an unsatisfactory transition between line 71/72 – whether finding a full stop after 'body', or reading 'Let' in his copy, as opposed to 'Lest'. This edition follows the emendations proposed by the great eighteenth-century editor of Shakespeare, Edward Capell, which addresses the one vulnerable spot in the Quarto text, and removes the incoherence at every level: grammatically, it turns lines 72–5 into a dependent clause of lines 66–71 and, structurally, it restores to Marcus at the end of the play the conciliatory public role he established at its start.

72   *bane* destruction

76   *frosty . . . chaps* white hair and cold cracks in the skin

78   *Cannot . . . words* Perhaps another outburst of commotion prompts him to cede the podium to Lucius.

79   *erst* once
        our ancestor Aeneas, who related the fall of Troy to Dido in Virgil's *Aeneid* II

84   *Sinon* A relation of Ulysses, he allowed himself to be taken prisoner by the Trojans and persuaded them to accept the Wooden Horse – the 'fatal engine' of the next line – into the city.

86   *civil wound* the mutilation of the body politic, civil war.

Marcus implies that the insertion of Tamora into the
heart of the state is analogous to the Trojans' acceptance
of the Wooden Horse.

87   *compact* composed

89   *But* without

91   *ye* Marcus addressing Lucius, along with the Romans

92   *force . . . commiseration* Marcus claims that the misfor-
        tunes of the Andronici as told by Lucius will inevitably
        evoke pity, as much as the story of the fall of Troy told
        by Aeneas.

100   *and basely cozened* and he was despicably cheated

101   *fought . . . out* fought to the end

103–14 *Lastly . . . truth.* In *Coriolanus* Shakespeare returns to
        the exile of an uncompromising field commander, who,
        eventually, was forced out of Rome.

103   *unkindly* unnaturally

108   *turned-forth* the turned-out, the castaway

109–11 *That have . . . body.* Lucius reminds the Romans of his
        record of service in order to show that he has been
        ill-rewarded for it, and that his alliance with the Goths
        should not be taken as treachery.

111   *advent'rous* willing to incur risk

113–14 *My scars . . . truth.* The custom of showing scars and
        wounds in order to secure popular suffrage is also pivotal
        in *Coriolanus* II.2.136–9.

120   *irreligious* godless

125   *patience* Titus's excesses need explaining, as Patience –
        as opposed to revenge – was the acceptable moral stance
        against injury and adversity.

128   *Have we* if we have

133   *mutual closure* shared extinction

139   *The common . . . so.* This line is anticipated at IV.4. 69–
        77 and V.1.1–4.

148   *give me aim awhile* assist me for a while. This is an
        expression from archery where the archer is helped in
        target practice by an observer reporting where the pre-
        vious shaft has landed.

227

149   *puts me to a heavy task* imposes on me the burden of mourning

150–73 This episode of intimate grief contrasts with the formal obsequies and Alarbus's ritual sacrifice in I.1.

151   *obsequious* dutiful, but also pertaining to obsequies
       trunk corpse

156   *tenders* tender kisses, but also repayment of a duty, an image prolonged into a conceit by 'sum', 'pay' and 'countless' in lines 157–8

164–8 See An Account of the Text, p. 229.

172   *so* provided that

179   *cry for food* This terrible sentence has been anticipated at V.3.6. Aaron is to be executed by starvation.

181   *doom* See note to III.1.24.

194   *ravenous* rapacious, insatiable

195–9 The Romans' failure to grant Tamora a decent burial sheds a negative light on the new regime, which has just attempted to distinguish itself from the old one by replacing sacrifice and ritual obsequies with pity and compassion. See note to 150–73 above.

197   *to prey* to prey upon. Aaron is excommunicated from the ranks of the living, while Tamora becomes the food he lacks.

AN ACCOUNT OF THE TEXT

Titus Andronicus was first published in 1594 in a quarto edition (Q1) printed by John Danter. This is almost certainly the 'booke intituled a Noble Roman Historye of Tytus Andronicus' entered in the Stationers' Register by Danter on 6 February 1594.

There is no reason to doubt that Danter's edition was based on an authorial manuscript. Several aspects of Q1 suggest a direct link with Shakespeare's foul papers, that is, the state of the text before it reached the theatre, where it would be transcribed, normalized and used as a prompt-book. Most prominently, the stage directions in Q1 are sketchy and sparse; alternative speech prefixes are used to refer to the same character; and three passages at I.1.35–8, III.1.36 and IV.3.94–106 are sometimes regarded as afterthoughts, which Shakespeare failed to integrate with the scene or sequence within which they are embedded.

The Second Quarto (Q2) was set from a copy of Q1 and published in 1600. The corrector of Q2 omitted the first of the three passages mentioned above, tampered with the second, but left the last one unaltered. The corrector of Q2 was also responsible for replacing five original lines at V.3.164–8 with five new, spurious lines, for modifying the very last line of the play and for adding four new lines to the original ending. It was only in 1904, when the only extant copy of Q1 was discovered in Sweden, that editors realized that the corrector of Q2 must have been forced to compensate for extensive damage to the last two leaves in his copy of Q1 (see the collation of V.3 in the 'Rejected Emendations' list printed below). All editions subsequent to Q2 until the discovery of Q1 inherited the tampered ending, along with some accurate corrections of obvious compositorial mistakes in Q1.

The third Quarto (Q3) was published in 1611 and is a fairly

straightforward reprint of Q2. Q3 was used as copy-text for the First Folio in 1623 (F1), but only after being heavily annotated by comparison with a theatrical document, most probably a prompt-book, as the number and quality of the new stage directions introduced in F1 make clear. Besides more detailed and more accurate stage directions, F1 introduces act-breaks, a theatrical practice which first came into use around 1608. F1 drops five sound Quarto lines at II.1.101, IV.2.8, IV.2.76, V.2.160 and V.3.51, it adds a dubious line at I.1.403 and a similarly awkward half-line at IV.1.36, and provides a whole new episode at III.2, known as the 'Fly scene'. Although editors cannot establish the exact date of this addition, a remarkable consistency of imagery and diction suggests that it is almost certainly authorial. Internal evidence supports the hypothesis of a later addition. The previous scene, for example, concludes with a strong statement of the revenge motif of the Andronici, which is at once developed in IV.1; without III.2 the play retains an unbroken narrative line. Titus, Marcus, Lavinia and young Lucius leave the stage at the end of III.2 to reappear immediately at the start of IV.1, but the practice of exiting-to-return is not Shakespearean. Only in III.2 does Tamora appear as 'Tamira', and Titus as *Andronicus* in the stage directions, and as *An.* in the speech prefixes. The lines in III.2 are metrically and rhythmically freer than in the rest of the play, which might suggest that they were composed at a later date.

Given its direct link with the author's foul papers, Q1 is generally adopted as copy-text for modern scholarly editions of this early tragedy. The present edition is based on Q1, except for III.2, which is based on F1. This edition endorses the three dubious Q1 passages mentioned above, because, despite their hypothetical status as afterthoughts, they cause no significant disruption to the pattern of meaning and the pace of the surrounding dialogue. In the first passage at I.1.35–8, for example, Marcus announces that Titus has already sacrificed the noblest prisoner of the Goths. Later on in the same scene, however, Lucius obtains Titus's permission to sacrifice Alarbus, Tamora's eldest son, who is promptly dispatched off stage. As former editors have suggested, the opening of the first passage – 'and at this day' – might be interpreted as an allusion not to Alarbus's sacrifice, but to a ritual which Titus performs 'on such days as this one', that is on the days of his triumphant return to Rome from the wars against the Goths. Line 33 tells us that there have been five such days. 'Done' at line 37 would then parallel 'Five times he hath returned' at line 33 and read 'Five times hath he done sacrifice'. Lines 99–104 and 125–9 confirm that this ritual is well-established. Similarly, the metric awkwardness of the half-line in Titus's complaint at III.1.33–40 – 'And bootlesse vnto them' – can be justified as a symptom of Titus's progressive decline into madness, as opposed to Shakespeare's failure to delete a false start. The last controversial passage at IV.3.94–106, which is often believed to represent undeleted first thoughts in the foul papers, mainly on the grounds of a repetition, as Titus asks the Clown the same question at lines 97–8 and at line 106, also makes powerful dramatic sense. The Clown's first answer is a witty disclaimer of his rhetorical skills: to Titus's request, 'Tell me, can you deliver an oration to the Emperor with a grace?' (IV.3.97–8), the Clown replies that he cannot even say grace before dinner, let alone speak an oration. When Titus encounters further resistance, he asks the Clown to stop ('Hold, hold', IV.3.104) and offers him money. What could be more natural, therefore, than that Titus, having written the oration, should repeat in modified form the request originally resisted, and that he should now receive an affirmative answer?

Q1 is followed very closely in the present edition, and emended only when the other early texts or subsequent scholarly editions correct obvious compositorial mistakes. The original spelling and punctuation have been modernized, and the stage directions improved by resorting to F1 or to later editions. Jonathan Bate's Arden edition of *Titus Andronicus* (third series) and the innovative edition of *Titus Andronicus* included in Stanley Wells and Gary Taylor's *William Shakespeare: Complete Works* have proved particularly useful as a source of extensive new directions, which have greatly improved the reader's perception of the theatrical qualities of this play.

The following collations list the main departures from Q1, rejected emendations from earlier editions, stage directions which derive from a source other than Q1 and substantial emendations of the original punctuation in Q1, which affect meaning and/or lineation. Q and F indicate readings common to all Quarto and the Folio editions.

COLLATIONS

I

The collation printed below lists all departures from the First Quarto (Q1), except for stage directions and substantive emendations of the original punctuation and lineation, which are treated separately below. This list ignores corrections of misprints and modernization of archaic and obsolete spelling in Q1. The readings listed at III.2 represent departures from the First Folio (F1), as this scene does not appear in the earlier Quarto editions of 1594, 1600 and 1611. Origin is noted only when the source is a later Quarto or Folio edition. Eighteenth-century editors first introduced most of the other emendations listed below.

THE CHARACTERS IN THE PLAY] *not in* Q, F
I.1   6 wore] Q (ware)
       18 MARCUS] *not in* Q, F
       36 the Andronici] that Andronicy Q1; *not in* Q2–3, F
       44 Capitol] Q3, F; Capitall Q1–2
       67 CAPTAIN] F, *not in* Q
       74 freight] fraught Q, F
       81 rites] Q3, F; rights Q1–2
      101 *manes*] F3; *manus* Q, F1–2
      144 these] the Q, F
      146 rites] F2–4; rights Q1–3, F1
      160 LAVINIA] *not in* Q1–2; Laui. Q3, F
      229 Titan's] Q2–3, F (Tytans); Tytus Q1

245 Pantheon] F3–4; Pathan Q, F1; Panthaeon F2

267 chance] Q2–3, F; change Q1

283 *cuique*] F2–4; *cuiqum* Q1–2; *cuiquam* Q3, F1

319 Phoebe] F2–4; *Thebe* Q, F1

361 MARTIUS *and* QUINTUS] *Titus two sonnes speakes.*
    Q, F1–2; *Titus two sonnes speak* F3–4

363 MARTIUS] *Titus sonne speakes.* Q, F

371 QUINTUS] *3. Sonne* Q; *1. Sonne* F

372 MARTIUS] *2. Sonne* Q, F

374 MARTIUS] *2. Sonne* Q, F

399 beholden] beholding Q, F

401 MARCUS] *not in* Q; F *continues to Titus*
    Yes, and will nobly him remunerate.] F; *not in* Q

408 seize] F2–4; ceaze Q; cease F1

454 raze] F3–4; race Q1–3, F1–2

477 LUCIUS] *not in* Q; *Son.* F

II.1   26 years want] F2–4; yeares wants Q, F1

       110 than] this Q, F

       122 with all] withall Q1

II.2   1 morn] Q3, F; Moone Q1–2

        24 run] F2–4; runnes Q1–3, F1

II.3   69 try experiments] Q2–3, F; trie thy experimens Q1

        72 swart] swartie Q1–2; swarty Q3; swarth F
           Cimmerian] F2–4; Cymerion Q, F1

        85 note] notice Q, F

        95 O'ercome] Q2–3, F (Orecome); Ouercome Q1

       107 yew] F; Ewghe Q1; Ewgh Q2; Ewe Q3

       110 Lascivious] Q3, F; Lauicious Q1–2

       126 quaint] painted Q, F

       131 ye] F2–4; we Q, F1

       144 sucked'st] suckst Q, F

       150 heard] Q2–3, F; hard Q1

       160 ears] Q3, F1–4; yeares Q1–2

       192 AARON] F; *not in* Q

       210 unhallowed] F (vnhallow'd); vnhollow Q

       222 berayed in blood] bereaud in blood Q1; embrewed
           heere Q2–3, F; heere reav'd of lyfe *early MS*

emendation in the margin of the sole surviving copy of Q1

	231	Pyramus] Q2–3, F (Piramus); Priamus Q1
	236	Cocytus] F2–4 (Cocitus); *Ocitus* Q, F1
	260	grieved] Q2–3, F (greeu'd | grieu'd); griude Q1
	291	proved] proud Q1
II.4	11	MARCUS] *not in* Q, F
	27	him] them Q, F
	30	three] their Q, F
	39	sewed] F3–4; sowed Q, F1–2
	43	sewed] F4; sowed Q, F1–3
III.1	9	are] F2–4; is Q, F1
	12	these two,] these, Q, F1; these, these F2–3; these, these, F4; these, good
	21	on thy] Q1 (outhy)
	67	handless] Q2–3, F; handles Q1
	146	his true] F4; her true Q, F1–3
	169	Writing] F; Wrighting Q
	215	sorrows] sorrow Q, F
	224	blow] F2–4; flow Q, F1
	280	employèd:] imployde in these Armes, Q; employd in these things: F
III.2	1–85	*This scene does not appear in* Q, *see An Account of the Text above.*
	1	TITUS] An. F *(throughout scene)*
	13	with outrageous] F2–4; without ragious F1
	39	complainer] complaynet F1; complaint F2–4
	52	thy knife] F2–4; knife F1
	53	fly] F2–4; Flys F1
	54	thee] F3–4; the F1–2
	55	are cloyed] F2–4; cloi'd F1
	72	myself] F2–4; my selfes F1
IV.1	1	YOUNG LUCIUS] Puer Q; Boy F *(throughout scene)*
	10	MARCUS] *not in* Q, F
	19	griefs] Q3, F; greeues Q1–2
	50	quotes] Q2–3, F; coats Q1
	53	Forced] Q2–3, F (Forc'd); Frocd Q1

	77	TITUS] *not in* Q1–2; *at line* 78 *in* Q3, F
	87	hope] Q2–3, F; h op Q1 (*slipped to the edge of the page*)
	90	swore] sweare Q, F1–2; sware F3–4
	122	good man] Q2–3, F; goodman Q1
IV.2	15	that,] *not in* Q, F
	51	Good] Q3, F; God Q1–2
	68	fair-faced] fairefast Q1–2; fairest Q3, F
	94	Alcides] Q2–3, F; *Alciades* Q1
	95	seize] F3–4; ceaze Q, F1–2
	123	that] Q3, F; your Q1–2
	151	Muly lives] *Muliteus* Q, F
IV.3	32	But [ ]] But *catchword* Q1; *omitted in* Q2–3, F. *A line or more may be missing here.*
	45	Acheron] F2–4; Acaron Q, F1
	54	*Apollinem*] *Apollonem* Q, F2–4; *Appollonem* F1
	57	Saturn', Caius] *Saturnine*, *to Caius* Q, F
	66	aimed] aim Q, F
	67	Jupiter] Q2–3, F; *Iubiter* Q1; *also at lines* 79 *and* 83
	77	News, . . . come.] F; *2 lines in* Q1, *assigned to Clowne*; *2 lines in* Q2–3, *assigned to Titus*
	116	must hold] hast made Q, F
IV.4	5	know, as know] know Q, F
	48	by'Lady] Q (be Lady), F (berLady)
	93	feed] Q3; seede Q1–2; foode F
	98	ears] F; yeares Q
	113	incessantly] sucessantly Q1; successantly Q2–3, F
V.1	9	FIRST GOTH] *Goth* Q, F
	17	ALL THE GOTHS] F2–4 (*Omn.*); Q, F1 *continue to Goth*
	20	SECOND GOTH] *Goth* Q, F
	27	dam] Q2–3, F; dame Q1
	43	here's] Q2–3, F; her's Q1
	53	Get me a ladder] *assigned to Aaron in* Q, F
	84	nurse] nourish Q, F
	133	haystacks] F (Haystackes); haystalks Q1; haystakes Q2–3

V.2 18 give it action] F; giue that accord Q1–3; give it that accord

    38 them out] Q2–3, F; the mout Q1

    49 globe] Globes Q, F

    52 murderers] murder Q, F

      caves] F2–4; cares Q, F1

    56 Hyperion's] F4 (*Hiperion's*); *Epeons* Q; *Eptons* F1; *Hiperions* F2; *Hiperious* F3

    61 Are they] F2–4; Are them Q, F1

    65 worldly] Q2–3, F; wordly Q1

V.3 26 gracious] Q2–3, F; *not in* Q

  72–94 *continued to Marcus*] *attributed to* Romane Lord *in* Q, *and to* Goth *in* F; *in* F4, *lines 76–94 are spoken by Marcus*

    93 Here's] Her's Q1; Heere is Q2–3, F

   124 cause] F4; course Q, F1–3

 140, 145 ROMANS] *attributed to Marcus in* Q, F

   153 bloodstained] F3–4 (blood-stain'd); blood slaine Q1–2; bloud-slaine Q3, F

   195 rite] Q3, F; right Q1–2

2

Rejected Emendations

The following list includes some of the more interesting and important variant readings and proposed emendations *not* accepted in the present edition. They derive from the early editions (the three Quartos of 1594, 1600 and 1611 and the four Folios of 1623, 1632, 1663 and 1685) and from scholarly editions from the eighteenth century to the present. Provenance is noted only when emendations derive from the early editions. This list ignores obvious misprints and compositorial mistakes and/or tampering with verse and syntax, which slipped into every new early edition, while old misprints and inaccuracies inherited from Q1 were being progressively emended and normalized.

I.1   5   am his] was the F
        5–6   that was the last | That] of him that last F4
        35–8   and at this day . . . of the Goths.] *not in* Q2–3, F
         43   succeed] succeeded
         74   his] her F4
       102   earthy] earthly F
       141   his] her
       157   drugs] grudgges Q3, grudges F
       220   people's] Noble F
       307   none] there none els F2–4
II.1   18   servile] idle Q3, F
        26   wits wants] wit wants Q2–3, F
        64   jet] set F
        73   meaner] better F3–4
      101   *not in* F
II.3   20   yellowing] yelping F
        88   Why, I have] Why I haue F1; Why haue I F2–4
     115   be ye not henceforth] be not henceforth; be ye not
            from henceforth; be ye not henceforward
     120   the] thy Q3, F
     229   earthy] earthly Q3, F
II.4   15   an] in Q2–3, F
        21   half] have
        38   Philomela] Philomel
III.1   17   ruins] urns
        34   if] or if Q2–3; oh if F
           did mark] did heare F
        35   They would . . . I must,] *not in* Q3
      35–6   yet plead . . . unto them.] *not in* F
        37   sorrows] sorrowes bootles Q3, F
        59   agèd] noble Q3, F
     125   like] in Q2–3, F
     169   castle] casque; cask; crest
     229   her] their
     281   thy teeth] thine arms
III.2   1–85   *This scene does not appear in Q, see An Account of the Text above.*

237

	60	a father and mother] a father and a mother; father, brother
	62	doings] dolings; dronings; dotings; dirges
IV.1	36	F *adds* 'What booke?' *as a separate line*
	45	so] see how
IV.2	8	*not in* F
	9–17	*continued to* Demetrius *in* F1; *attributed to* Boy *in* F2
	71	Zounds, ye] Out you F
	76	*not in* F
	177	feed] fat; feast
IV.3	8	catch] finde Q3, F
	40	so] now
IV.4	18	unjustice] injustice F
	67	this] his
	78	your] our F
	102	*not in* Q3, F
V.1	46	deaf? Not a word?] deaf? no! Not a word? F2–4; deaf? What, not a word?
	141	But] Tut Q2–3, F
V.2	22	witness these] these
	71	humours] Q1 (humors); fits Q2–3, F
	160	*not in* F
V.3	51	*not in* F
	92	And force you to] Lending your kind Q2–3; Lending your kind hand F
	93	Rome's young] a Q2–3, F
	94	While I stand by] Your harts will throb Q2–3, F
	95	Then, gracious] Then noble Q2–3; This Noble F
	96	Chiron and the damned] cursed Chiron and Q2–3, F
	129	pleading] now Q2–3, F
	131	hurl ourselves] cast vs downe Q2–3, F
	132	souls] braines Q2–3, F
	163	story] matter Q2–3, F
	164–8	And bid thee ... | their latest kiss,] Meete and agreeing with thine infancie, | In that respect then,

like a louing child. (*comma in* Q3, F) | Shed yet
some small drops from thy tender spring, |
Because kind nature doth require it so, | Friends
should associate friends in griefe and woe. Q2–3,
F

175   A ROMAN] Romans F

199   dead . . . pity.] so, shall haue like want of pitty. |
See iustice done on Aron that damn'd Moore, |
By (From *in* F1, F3–4; For *in* F2) whom our
heauie haps had their beginning: | Than (Then *in*
Q3, F) afterwards to order well the state, | That
like euents may nere it ruinate. Q2–3, F

3

Stage Directions

The collation printed below lists substantive departures from the
stage directions as they appear in Q1. Stage directions in Q1 are
notoriously sparse and inadequate. Supplementary directions
have therefore been added to clarify the action. The origin of
additional directions is indicated only when their source is F.
The alterations listed at III.2 represent departures from the First
Folio (F1), as this scene does not appear in the earlier Quarto
editions of 1594, 1600 and 1611. Minor editorial interventions,
such as the addition of 'asides' or the name of the addressee of a
specific speech or specific lines within a longer speech, are not
noted. Q2–3 and F2–4 are not collated separately, unless their
stage directions are used in the present edition, as at I.1.294 or
II.3.208.

I.1   0   *Flourish. Enter the tribunes and senators aloft; and
then enter below Saturninus and his followers at one
door, and Bassianus and his followers at the other,
with drums and colours*] Enter the Tribunes *and*
Senatours *aloft: And then enter* Saturninus *and his
followers at one dore, and* Bassianus *and his followers,
with Drums and Trumpets.* Q1; *Flourish. Enter the*

239

I.1   0   *Tribunes and Senators aloft. And then enter Satur-*
             ninus and his Followers at one doore, and Bassianus
             and his Followers at the other, with Drum & Colours.
             F

        17   *Enter Marcus Andronicus aloft with the crown*] F;
             Marcus Andronicus with the Crowne. Q

        58   *Exeunt his soldiers; his other followers remain*] *Exit*
             Soldiers. Q, F

        62   *not in* Q, F

        66   *Flourish*] *not in* Q

        72   *three sons, Alarbus, Chiron and Demetrius,*] *two*
             sonnes Chiron *and* Demetrius, Q, F

       107   *not in* Q, F

       132   *Exeunt Titus's sons with Alarbus*] *Exit Titus sonnes*
             with Alarbus. Q; *Exit sonnes with Alarbus.* F

       133   *not in* Q, F

       144   *Enter the sons of Andronicus, with their swords bloody*]
             Enter the sonnes of Andronicus againe. Q, F

       164   *not in* Q, F

       171   *not in* Q, F

       172   *not in* Q, F

       205   *not in* Q, F

       215   *not in* Q, F

       223   *not in* Q, F

       236   *A long flourish till Marcus, Saturninus, Bassianus,*
             tribunes and senators come down. Marcus crowns
             Saturninus] *not in* Q; *A long Flourish till they come*
             downe. F

       278   *not in* Q, F

       279   *not in* Q, F

       285   *not in* Q, F

       289   *not in* Q, F

       291   *not in* Q, F

       292   *not in* Q, F

       294   *He attacks Mutius*] *not in* Q, F

       295   *Titus kills him*] *not in* Q1–2; *He kills him.* Q3, F

       301   *Exit*] *not in* Q, F

340 *Exeunt all but Titus*] *Exeunt omnes.* Q, F

386 *not in* Q, F

392 *kneeling*] *They all kneel and say,* Q, F

393 *They rise*] *not in* Q, F

Exeunt all but Marcus and Titus] *Exit all but Marcus and Titus.* Q, F

401 *Flourish. Enter the Emperor, Tamora and her two sons, with the Moor, at one door. Enter at the other door Bassianus and Lavinia, with Lucius, Quintus and Martius*] *Enter the Emperour, Tamora and her two sonnes, with the Moore at one doore. Enter at the other doore Bascianus and Lauinia, with others.* Q; *Flourish. Enter the Emperor, Tamora, and her two sons, with the Moore at one doore. Enter at the other doore Bassianus and Lauinia with others.* F

429 *not in* Q, F

463 *not in* Q, F

476 *not in* Q, F

480 *not in* Q, F

488 *not in* Q, F

498 *Sound trumpets. Exeunt all but Aaron*] *Exeunt. Sound trumpets, manet* Moore. Q; *Exeunt.* | *Actus Secunda* F

II.1 0 *Aaron is alone on stage*] *not in* Q; *Flourish. Enter Aaron alone.* F

II.2 0 *Enter Marcus, Titus Andronicus and his three sons, Lucius, Quintus, and Martius, making a noise with hounds and horns*] *Enter* Titus Andronicus, *and his three sonnes. making a noise with hounds & hornes.* Q; *Enter Titus Andronicus and his three sonnes, making a noise with hounds and hornes, and Marcus.* F

II.3 0 *with gold*] *not in* Q, F

7 *not in* Q, F

45 *not in* Q, F

54 *not in* Q, F

116 *He stabs Bassanius*] *stab him* Q, F

117 *not in* Q, F

168 *not in* Q, F
184 *not in* Q, F
186 *not in* Q, F
187 *not in* Q, F1; *Exeunt* F2, *after* 186
191 *Exit*] F; *not in* Q
     Quintus and Martius] *not in* Q, F
197 *not in* Q, F
208 *Exit*] Q2–3; *after* 207 *in* Q1; *Exit Aron.* F
245 *He falls in*] *not in* Q; *Boths fall in* F
     with attendants] *not in* Q, F
268 SATURNINUS (*reads*)] *Saturninus reads the letter.* Q,
     F
285 *not in* Q, F
288 *not in* Q, F
299 *not in* Q, F
303 *not in* Q, F
306 *Exeunt with Martius and Quintus under guard, and
     attendants with the body of Bassianus*] *not in* Q;
     Exeunt F

II.4   10 *Wind horns. Enter Marcus from hunting to Lavinia*]
             F; *Enter Marcus from hunting.* Q

III.1   0 *tribunes as*] *not in* Q, F
             over] *on* Q, F
         16 *Exeunt the judges and others with the prisoners*] *not
             in* Q; *Exeunt* F
         52 *not in* Q, F
         64 *not in* Q, F
         65 *not in* Q, F
        138 *not in* Q, F
        190 *left hand*] *hand* Q, F
        205 *not in* Q, F
        208 *not in* Q, F
        232 *Titus and Lavinia rise*] *not in* Q, F
        239 *Exit, after setting down the heads and hand*] *not in*
             Q1; *Exit* Q2–3, F
        248 *not in* Q, F
        277 *not in* Q, F

286 *They kiss] not in* Q, F
    Exeunt all but Lucius] Exeunt. Q; *Exeunt. Manet*
    Lucius F

III.2 1–85 *This scene does not appear in* Q. *See An Account of*
    the Text, above.

    3 *not in* F

    11 *not in* F

    75 *not in* F

IV.1 0 *Young Lucius]* F; *Lucius sonne* Q

    4 *not in* Q, F

    29 *not in* Q, F

    64 *not in* Q, F

    69 *at 67 in* Q, F

    87 *not in* Q, F

    93 *not in* Q, F

IV.2 13 *not in* Q, F

    17 *Exit with attendant] Exit.* Q, F

    86 *not in* Q, F

    133 *not in* Q, F

    145 *not in* Q, F

    161 *not in* Q, F

    170 *Exeunt Chiron and Demetrius with the Nurse's body]*
    Exeunt. Q, F

IV.3 0 *Enter* Titus, *old Marcus, his son Publius, young*
    Lucius, and other gentlemen (Caius, Sempronius)
    with bows, and Titus bears the arrows with letters on
    the ends of them] Enter Titus, *olde* Marcus, *young*
    Lucius, *and other gentlemen with bowes, and* Titus
    beares the arrowes with letters on the ends of them.
    Q1; *Enter Titus, old Marcus, young Lucius, and other*
    gentlemen with bowes, and Titus beares the arrowes
    with Letters on the end of them. F

    64 *not in* Q, F

    104 *not in* Q, F

    105 *not in* Q, F

    108 *not in* Q, F

    114 *not in* Q, F

IV.4   0   *Chiron . . . attendants.*] *not in* Q, F
        34 *(Aside)*] *not in* Q; *at end of line 35 in* F
        49 *Exit guarded*] *Exit* Q, F
        60 *Aemilius, a messenger*] *Nutius Emillius* Q

V.1   0 *Flourish*] F; *not in* Q
        19 *leading*] F2–4; *leading of* Q, F1
        53 *not in* Q, F
      146 *not in* Q, F
      151 *Aaron is gagged*] *not in* Q, F
      165 *Flourish*] *at the end of line 164 in* F; *not in* Q
           Exeunt] Q3, F; *not in* Q1–2

V.2   0 *Enter Tamora disguised as Revenge, and her two sons, Chiron as Rape and Demetrius as Murder*] *Enter Tamora and her two sonnes disguised.* Q, F
        8 *above*] *not in* Q, F
       69 *not in* Q, F
       80 *not in* Q, F
      121 *at the end of line 120 in* Q, F
      131 *not in* Q, F
      148 *not in* Q, F
      151 *not in* Q, F
      160 *not in* Q, F
      162 *not in* Q, F
      204 *with the bodies*] *not in* Q, F

V.3   0 *with Aaron prisoner, and his child*] *not in* Q, F
       15 *Flourish*] F; *not in* Q
       16 *Exeunt Goths with Aaron*] *not in* Q, F
           Aemilius] *not in* Q, F
       25 *Trumpets sounding. A table brought in. They sit. Enter Titus like a cook, placing the dishes, and Lavinia with a veil over her face, with young Lucius and others*] *Trumpets sounding. Enter Titus like a Cooke, placing the dishes, and Lauinia with a vaile ouer her face.* Q; *Hoboyes. A Table brought in. Enter Titus like a Cooke, placing the meat on the Table, and Lauinia with a vale ouer her face.* F
       44 *not in* Q, F

46   *He kills her*] Q3, F; *not in* Q1–2
63   *not in* Q, F
65   *not in* Q, F
66   *not in* Q, F
75   *not in* Q, F
118 *not in* Q, F
144 *not in* Q, F
151 *not in* Q, F
155 *not in* Q, F

4

Punctuation and Lineation

This collation lists substantive emendations of the original punctuation and lineation, but ignores incidental alterations in the
punctuation which leave the original sense unaltered. The alterations listed at III.2 represent departures from the First Folio
(F1), as this scene does not appear in the earlier Quarto editions
of 1594, 1600 and 1611.

I.1   14   seat, to virtue consecrate,] seate to vertue, con-
            secrate Q; seate to Vertue: consecrate F
       206 *2 lines in* Q, F
       288 *2 lines in* Q, F
     293–4 *What . . . Rome?*] *1 line in* Q, F
       336 queen, Pantheon. Lords, accompany] Queene:
            Panthean Lords accompany Q; Qeene, | Panthean
            Lords, accompany F
     488–9 *1 line in* Q, F
II.1   4–8 reach. . . . hills,] reach, . . . hills. Q; reach: . . . hills:
            F
       45   *2 lines in* Q, F
     79–80 Aaron . . . deaths | . . . propose to . . . love.] Aaron
            . . . deaths . . . propose, | To . . . loue. Q, F
       97   *2 lines in* Q, F
       102 *2 lines in* Q, F
II.2 16–17 I say no: . . . more] F; *1 line in* Q

20 *2 lines in* Q, F

II.3 132 outlive, us] out liue us Q1; out-liue vs Q2–3, F

184–5 Nay then . . . her husband.] F; *1 line in* Q

III.1 63 *2 lines in* Q, F

176 *2 lines in* Q, F

184 *2 lines in* Q, F

III.2 65 *2 lines in* F

66 *2 lines in* F

74–5 *1 line in* F

IV.1 95–9 beware: | The . . . once. | She's . . . league, | And . . . back, | And, . . . list.] beware, | The . . . once, | Shee's . . . league, | And . . . backe. | And . . . list. Q; beware | The . . . once, | Shee's . . . league. | And . . . backe, | And . . . list. F

IV.2 20–21 *1 line in* Q; *2 lines (prose) in* F

51–2 Good morrow, lords. | . . . the Moor?] F; *1 line in* Q

62 *2 lines in* Q, F

64–5 *1 line in* Q, F

80 *2 lines in* Q, F

168–9 Aaron . . . secrets.] *1 line in* Q, F

IV.3 7–8 *1 line in* Q, F

77 News, . . . come.] F; *2 lines in* Q1, *assigned to Clowne*; *2 lines in* Q2–3, *assigned to Titus*

84–5 Alas sir, . . . life.] *2 lines (verse) in* Q, F

89 From . . . there.] *verse in* Q, F

IV.4 36–7 quick: . . . out,] quick, . . . out: Q, F

V.1 95–6 Why, . . . and 'twas | Trim . . . doing of it.] Why . . . trimd, | And twas trim . . . doing of it. Q, F

V.2 152 *2 lines in* Q, F

V.3 28 all. Although] *after* F (all: although); all although Q

39 *2 lines in* Q, F

71 body,] body. Q, F

72 herself,] her selfe. Q, F

124 revenge] F; reuenge. Q

READ MORE IN PENGUIN

In every corner of the world, on every subject under the sun, Penguin represents quality and variety – the very best in publishing today.

For complete information about books available from Penguin – including Puffins, Penguin Classics and Arkana – and how to order them, write to us at the appropriate address below. Please note that for copyright reasons the selection of books varies from country to country.

In the United Kingdom: Please write to *Dept. EP, Penguin Books Ltd, Bath Road, Harmondsworth, West Drayton, Middlesex UB7 ODA*

In the United States: Please write to *Consumer Sales, Penguin Putnam Inc., P.O. Box 12289 Dept. B, Newark, New Jersey 07101-5289.* VISA and MasterCard holders call 1-800-788-6262 to order Penguin titles

In Canada: Please write to *Penguin Books Canada Ltd, 10 Alcorn Avenue, Suite 300, Toronto, Ontario M4V 3B2*

In Australia: Please write to *Penguin Books Australia Ltd, P.O. Box 257, Ringwood, Victoria 3134*

In New Zealand: Please write to *Penguin Books (NZ) Ltd, Private Bag 102902, North Shore Mail Centre, Auckland 10*

In India: Please write to *Penguin Books India Pvt Ltd, 11 Community Centre, Panchsheel Park, New Delhi 110017*

In the Netherlands: Please write to *Penguin Books Netherlands bv, Postbus 3507, NL-1001 AH Amsterdam*

In Germany: Please write to *Penguin Books Deutschland GmbH, Metzlerstrasse 26, 60594 Frankfurt am Main*

In Spain: Please write to *Penguin Books S. A., Bravo Murillo 19, 1° B, 28015 Madrid*

In Italy: Please write to *Penguin Italia s.r.l., Via Benedetto Croce 2, 20094 Corsico, Milano*

In France: Please write to *Penguin France, Le Carré Wilson, 62 rue Benjamin Baillaud, 31500 Toulouse*

In Japan: Please write to *Penguin Books Japan Ltd, Kaneko Building, 2-3-25 Koraku, Bunkyo-Ku, Tokyo 112*

In South Africa: Please write to *Penguin Books South Africa (Pty) Ltd, Private Bag X14, Parkview, 2122 Johannesburg*

RSC
ROYAL
SHAKESPEARE
COMPANY

The Royal Shakespeare Company today is probably one of the best known theatre companies in the world, playing regularly to audiences of more than a million people a year. The RSC has three theatres in Stratford-upon-Avon, the Royal Shakespeare Theatre, the Swan Theatre and The Other Place, and two theatres in London's Barbican Centre, the Barbican Theatre and The Pit. The Company also has an annual season in Newcastle-upon-Tyne and regularly undertakes tours throughout the UK and overseas.

Find out more about the RSC and its current repertoire by joining the Company's mailing list. Not only will you receive advance information of all the Company's activities, but also priority booking, special ticket offers, copies of the RSC Magazine and special offers on RSC publications and merchandise.

If you would like to receive details of the Company's work and an application form for the mailing list please write to:

RSC Membership Office
Royal Shakespeare Theatre
FREEPOST
Stratford-upon-Avon
CV37 6BR

or telephone: 01789 205301

READ MORE IN PENGUIN

LITERARY CRITICISM

The Penguin History of Literature

Published in ten volumes, *The Penguin History of Literature* is a superb critical survey of the English and American literature covering fourteen centuries, from the Anglo-Saxons to the present, and written by some of the most distinguished academics in their fields.

New Bearings in English Poetry F. R. Leavis

'*New Bearings in English Poetry* was the first intelligent account of the work of Eliot, Pound and Gerard Manley Hopkins to appear in English and it significantly altered critical awareness . . . Leavis gave to literary criticism a thoroughness and respectability that has never since been equalled' Peter Ackroyd, *Spectator*. 'The most influential literary critic of modern times' *Financial Times*

The Uses of Literacy Richard Hoggart

Mass literacy has opened new worlds to new readers. How far has it also been exploited to debase standards and behaviour? 'A vivid inside view of working-class culture and one of the most influential books of the post-war era' *Observer*

Epistemology of the Closet Eve Kosofsky Sedgwick

Through her brilliant interpretation of the readings of Henry James, Melville, Nietzsche, Proust and Oscar Wilde, Eve Kosofsky Sedgwick shows how questions of sexual definition are at the heart of every form of representation in this century. 'A signal event in the history of late-twentieth-century gay studies' Wayne Koestenbaum

Dangerous Pilgrimages Malcolm Bradbury

'This capacious book tracks Henry James from New England to Rye; Evelyn Waugh to a Hollywood as grotesque as he expected; Gertrude Stein to Spain to be mistaken for a bishop; Oscar Wilde to a rickety stage in Leadsville, Colorado . . . The textbook on the the the transatlantic theme' *Guardian*

READ MORE IN PENGUIN

LITERARY CRITICISM

The Practice of Writing   David Lodge

This lively collection examines the work of authors ranging from the two Amises to Nabokov and Pinter; the links between private lives and published works; and the different techniques required in novels, stage plays and screenplays. 'These essays, so easy in manner, so well-built and informative, offer a fine blend of creative writing and criticism' *Sunday Times*

A Lover's Discourse   Roland Barthes

'May be the most detailed, painstaking anatomy of desire we are ever likely to see or need again ... The book is an ecstatic celebration of love and language ... readers interested in either or both ... will enjoy savouring its rich and dark delights' *Washington Post*

The New Pelican Guide to English Literature   Edited by Boris Ford

The indispensable critical guide to English and American literature in nine volumes, erudite yet accessible. From the ages of Chaucer and Shakespeare, via Georgian satirists and Victorian social critics, to the leading writers of the twentieth century, all literary life is here.

The Structure of Complex Words   William Empson

'Twentieth-century England's greatest critic after T. S. Eliot, but whereas Eliot was the high priest, Empson was the *enfant terrible* ... *The Structure of Complex Words* is one of the linguistic masterpieces of the epoch, finding in the feel and tone of our speech whole sedimented social histories' *Guardian*

Vamps and Tramps   Camille Paglia

'Paglia is a genuinely unconventional thinker ... Taken as a whole, the book gives an exceptionally interesting perspective on the last thirty years of intellectual life in America, and is, in its wacky way, a celebration of passion and the pursuit of truth' *Sunday Telegraph*

READ MORE IN PENGUIN

CRITICAL STUDIES

Described by *The Times Educational Supplement* as 'admirable' and 'superb', Penguin Critical Studies is a specially developed series of critical essays on the major works of literature for use by students in universities, colleges and schools.

Titles published or in preparation include:

The Alchemist
The Poetry of William Blake
Critical Theory
Dickens's Major Novels
Doctor Faustus
Dombey and Son
Frankenstein
Great Expectations
The Great Gatsby
Heart of Darkness
The Poetry of Gerard
   Manley Hopkins
The Poetry of Keats
Mansfield Park
The Mayor of Casterbridge

Middlemarch
Paradise Lost
The Poetry of Alexander Pope
Rosencrantz and Guildenstern
   are Dead
Sense and Sensibility
Sons and Lovers
Tennyson
Tess of the D'Urbervilles
To the Lighthouse
The Waste Land
Wordsworth
Wuthering Heights
The Poetry of W. B. Yeats

READ MORE IN PENGUIN

CRITICAL STUDIES

Described by *The Times Educational Supplement* as 'admirable' and 'superb', Penguin Critical Studies is a specially developed series of critical essays on the major works of literature for use by students in universities, colleges and schools.

Titles published or in preparation include:

SHAKESPEARE

As You Like It
Hamlet
King Lear
Macbeth
The Merchant of Venice
A Midsummer Night's Dream
Much Ado about Nothing
Othello
Shakespeare's History Plays
The Taming of the Shrew
The Tempest
Twelfth Night
The Winter's Tale

CHAUCER

Chaucer
The Prologue to
  The Canterbury Tales

READ MORE IN PENGUIN

THE NEW PENGUIN SHAKESPEARE

All's Well That Ends Well	Barbara Everett
Antony and Cleopatra	Emrys Jones
As You Like It	H. J. Oliver
The Comedy of Errors	Stanley Wells
Coriolanus	G. R. Hibbard
Hamlet	T. J. B. Spencer
Henry IV, Part 1	P. H. Davison
Henry IV, Part 2	P. H. Davison
Henry V	A. R. Humphreys
Henry VI, Parts 1–3	Norman Sanders
(three volumes)	
Henry VIII	A. R. Humphreys
Julius Caesar	Norman Sanders
King John	R. L. Smallwood
King Lear	G. K. Hunter
Love's Labour's Lost	John Kerrigan
Macbeth	G. K. Hunter
Measure for Measure	J. M. Nosworthy
The Merchant of Venice	W. Moelwyn Merchant
The Merry Wives of Windsor	G. R. Hibbard
A Midsummer Night's Dream	Stanley Wells
Much Ado About Nothing	R. A. Foakes
Othello	Kenneth Muir
Pericles	Philip Edwards
Richard II	Stanley Wells
Richard III	E. A. J. Honigmann
Romeo and Juliet	T. J. B. Spencer
The Sonnets and A Lover's Complaint	John Kerrigan
The Taming of the Shrew	G. R. Hibbard
The Tempest	Anne Barton
Timon of Athens	G. R. Hibbard
Troilus and Cressida	R. A. Foakes
Twelfth Night	M. M. Mahood
The Two Gentlemen of Verona	Norman Sanders
The Two Noble Kinsmen	N. W. Bawcutt
The Winter's Tale	Ernest Schanzer